D1286571

January 1986

86-57

02.5
I8
c.2

# GARDENING

# GARDENING
## *A Guide to the Literature*

Richard T. Isaacson

GARLAND PUBLISHING, INC. • NEW YORK & LONDON
1985

Ref
Z
5996
.A1
I8
1985

© 1985 Richard T. Isaacson
All rights reserved

**Library of Congress Cataloging-in-Publication Data**

Isaacson, Richard T.
  Gardening : a guide to the literature.

  Includes indexes.
  1. Gardening—Bibliography.   I. Title.
Z5996.A1I8   1985   [SB450.97]   016.635        83-49072
ISBN 0-8240-9019-5 (alk. paper)

Cover design by Jonathan Billing

Printed on acid-free, 250-year-life paper
Manufactured in the United States of America

# CONTENTS

# INTRODUCTION

Working with gardeners and building the collection of Eleanor Squire Library for the last twelve years have given me a keen appreciation of gardening literature and an admiration of the optimistic spirit of gardeners. This bibliography lists those materials (books, magazines, nursery and seed catalogs, etc.) that I have found to be of most use to gardeners.

To use this bibliography effectively it is important to understand its arrangement and scope. Thus, this introduction is brief and to the point. The bibliographic access to gardening literature is very limited. There are no good indexes or abstracts that gardeners can consult that access the majority of gardening literature. This bibliography was conceived as one source to consult when seeking information on the diverse world of gardening.

The compiler has accepted Liberty Hyde Bailey's definition of gardening as found in his gardening encyclopedia (45): "Gardening and horticulture are really synonymous terms, but, by usage, a horticulturist is supposed to have a more extended training and wider range of activities than a gardener. Moreover, the word gardening now suggests more of the private, homelike and personal point of view, whereas the most distinctive feature of American horticulture is [its] immense commercial importance." And, again to the point, I quote from *Hortus Third* (37): "The home garden should be useful in the degree to which it expresses the sentiments of its maker or owner; a garden planned without regard to personality may not fulfill the requisite. To accomplish essential results, the garden maker must be well prepared to meet the requirements of the plants and to defend them against injury, insect, and disease; to this end he must be informed by the latest bulletins and books on the subject." Thus, most materials relating to commercial horticulture, botany, landscape architecture, and natural history are beyond the scope of this selective bibliography. Also, guides to public gardens, plant lore, garden biographies, native plant guides, cookery, and many aspects of gardening history are not found here.

The arrangement of this bibliography is by broad subject areas as listed in the table of contents. General gardening works, reference titles, and reference titles from related disciplines are followed by a gardening plant breakdown, with gardening practices arranged last. It is most important to keep in mind that under each subject treatment the titles are arranged by the compiler's evaluation of their importance or effectiveness. The best titles are listed first, thus, for instance, under lilies the best introduction to the culture of lilies is the first title discussed.

Other aspects of this bibliography should be noted:

1. Books written for gardeners are given precedence over those texts which have a more botanical or commercial horticulture content.

2. Gardening literature written for American gardeners is generally of more value than those books written for gardeners in other countries. This is especially true of the many excellent English publications that are also published in this country.

3. Most gardening literature written in the United States has a bias towards the gardening conditions found in Northeastern or Eastern United States. Because of this bias, the compiler has attempted to include guides to gardening and the plants used in gardening in other North American geographic areas. Canadian gardeners will also find information of merit included.

4. Practical gardening information is more important than just a listing of plants. (For instance, a book on growing lilies is listed first, that is, rated higher, than a book that simply lists the many available lilies.)

5. This bibliography was written with the general gardener in mind. Gardeners who specialize only in a few plants or in one type of gardening will find less of worth here than a gardener with more general interests. Under each topic, I first list a good title that introduces a subject to a novice gardener and then indicate other titles of interest to more experienced gardeners.

6. There is a bias towards more current literature in this bibliography as opposed to materials of mainly historical importance. Also in most instances the most recent edition and publisher are listed.

7. Many aspects of gardening deserve more detailed bibliographic treatment than they are given here. Because of space limitations, such subjects as flower arrangement, children's gardening, etc., are only introduced.

8. The length of the annotation does not necessarily reflect worth, but ranking does (the best book is discussed first).

9. The number of annotations in each section does not indicate relative importance. For instance, there are many more books listed on herb gardening than on vegetable gardening. This is not to say that herb gardening is more important than vegetable gardening, only that the literature on herbs is more abundant, etc.

10. Some of the most valuable sources of information for gardeners are not listed in this bibliography, especially local county extension-type publications. Information for local conditions, recommended pest and disease controls, and recommended plant varieties are found in these publications. These materials are designed to be easy for gardeners to use, and they emphasize current information. Most gardening reference sources list these more local agencies state by state. Local offices of these agencies are often listed in telephone directories under state listings. Access to U.S. governmental publications is listed in this bibliography.

11. Books are listed first in this bibliography, but many times plant society publications, periodicals, and seed and nursery catalogs are as important (or more so) for finding information on many gardening subjects.

12. This bibliography ignores publications of rather transitory nature which are usually published in softcover. In this category are publications in the Sunset gardening series and the Ortho gardening series. Also for the most part, such excellent smaller guides as the Brooklyn Botanic Garden Handbooks (528) are omitted. Those libraries and individuals looking for brief and inexpensive gardening titles should keep these publications in mind.

13. Basic gardening terminology is often not defined. It is assumed users of this bibliography will be familiar with such gardening terms as hardiness, genus, species, forcing, etc. More specialized gardening terminology is avoided.

14. Foreign-language titles are ignored except for a few French titles from Canada.

15. Publication information listed includes publisher, place of publication, date, and where pertinent, pagination, series statement and U.S. distributor.

16. Although other libraries have been visited during the compilation of this bibliography, this bibliography is based on the compiler's knowledge and the collection of Eleanor Squire Library. Unless stated the compiler is familiar with items included. [Note: one title I have not seen or included but should be mentioned is: *The European Garden Flora*, currently being published in Cambridge, England. It is described as a multi-volume manual for the identification of plants cultivated in Europe, both out-of-doors and indoors. Volume two, the first volume published, is described as containing information on 17 families, 402 genera and 1663 species.]

A special mention should be made of seed and nursery catalogs. Listed in these catalogs is the most currently available plant material for gardeners. Gardeners cherish and religiously read these catalogs. Plants are historically often first listed in these catalogs, then appear in periodical literature and finally reach monographic literature. Access to new plant material and information on this material is often found only in trade catalogs. Because of this historical importance, the Council on Botanical and Horticultural Library (CBHL) is currently sponsoring efforts to give these historic catalogs bibliographic access and to emphasize their importance in tracing the history of gardening plants in North America.

There are many people to thank for help in the compilation of this bibliography. My parents, Olaf and Edna encouraged me in all ways and started my appreciation of plants. Among those who helped to proofread this bibliography and provided advice and support are James E. Walters, Jr., Mrs. Samuel Lamport, Mrs. Clara Belle Katalinas, Mrs. Helen Tramte, Mrs. Lee Buss, Mrs. Esther Greenberg, and Ina Vrugtman, librarian of the Royal Botanic Garden, who arranged for the extended loan of many Canadian gardening titles. My thanks also to Alexander A. Apanius, director of The Garden Center of Greater Cleveland, the Board of Trustees of The Garden Center, the former librarians of The Garden Center, and to the many people in Cleveland who have built and supported that fine gardening library, the Eleanor Squire Library.

Finally to quote (using C.H. Oldfather's translation (in the Loeb

Classical Library, Cambridge: Harvard U. Press, 1933) the first-century B.C. historian Diodorus of Sicily in his *History*, Book 1, "It is to be hoped that what we have done well may not be the object of envy, and that the matters wherein our knowledge is defective may receive correction at the hand of [the] more able."


Richard T. Isaacson
Cleveland, January 1985

# Gardening

# GARDENING REFERENCE

1. American Horticultural Society. NORTH AMERICAN
   HORTICULTURE: A REFERENCE GUIDE. New York:
   Scribner, 1982. 367p.
   This large, topically arranged directory lists
   such organizations as public gardens and arboreta,
   civic garden centers, plant societies, national
   horticultural organizations, plant nomenclature
   and international registration authorities, education programs, test and demonstration gardens, and
   more. The entries vary from brief addresses to
   long records detailing major institutions. Longer
   entries include address, telephone number,
   director or contact person, a description of
   collections, membership statistics, membership
   qualifications, publications, educational program,
   library collection, herbarium collection, and
   horticultural scholarships. The index should be
   used as information on specific organizations can
   be found in different parts of the directory.
   This directory is not arranged by state, so it is
   hard to compile listings on a particular state's
   or province's horticultural institutions. The most
   valuable directory of North American horticulture.

2. Massachusetts Horticultural Society. DICTIONARY
   CATALOG OF THE LIBRARY OF THE MASSACHUSETTS
   HORTICULTURAL SOCIETY. Boston: G.K. Hall, 1962.
   3 vols. 736,665,681p.
   FIRST SUPPLEMENT. Boston, G.K. Hall, 1972. 1 vol.
   441p.
   The printed card catalog of one of the great
   horticultural libraries of North America. The
   catalog and supplement include over 35,000 entries
   of materials published up to 1972. This
   library's collection is rich in early American
   books and periodicals. As with many historic
   collections, the level of cataloguing varies in
   accuracy and in depth. Since this dictionary

3

catalog was published, the library has sold a
portion of its historic European collection.

3.  Council on Botanical and Horticultural Libraries.
    DIRECTORY OF MEMBER LIBRARIES. Compiled by
    Bernadette G. Callery, Enola Jane Teeter, and
    Mary Lou Wolfe. Bronx, NY: author, 1983. 57p.
    The membership of this international specialized
    library organization is listed in this directory.
    Listing mainly North American libraries, it
    includes information such as address, telephone
    number, collection size, subject strengths, public
    services (hours, interlibrary loan policies,
    copying services), databases, staff, publications
    describing collections, and access through
    bibliographic utilities. There is a subject index
    to the libraries collections. Available through
    The Council on Botanical and Horticultural
    Libraries, c/o The New York Botanical Garden,
    Bronx, NY 10458.

4.  British Colour Council. HORTICULTURAL COLOUR CHART.
    London: British Colour Council/Royal Horticultural
    Society, 1938. 2 vols.
    These two volumes contain 200 charts that pinpoint
    exact color gradations. They are used to
    reference color in horticultural plants. The
    first edition contains names of colors (sulphur
    yellow, marigold orange) while a later, revised
    edition references only by color number. This
    work is out of print and much in demand.

5.  Huxley, Anthony. HUXLEY'S ENCYCLOPEDIA OF GARDENING
    FOR GREAT BRITAIN AND AMERICA. New York: Universe
    Books, 1982. 373p.
    "Bonsai," " growing point," " saprophyte," "harden-
    ing off," and "root vegetables" are among the
    common and uncommon gardening terms, processes,
    and plant parts defined in this title. This title
    has an English bias which can be useful when
    looking for definitions of English gardening
    terminology. Cross references are made to
    relevant entries. Conversion tables are given for
    metric/U.S. measurements.

6.  A TECHNICAL GLOSSARY OF HORTICULTURAL AND LANDSCAPE
    TERMINOLOGY. Washington, DC: Horticulture Research
    Institute, 1971. 109p.
    This glossary is a joint project of many
    professional and trade horticultural associations.
    Among terms found are "eminent domain," "rooting
    medium," "phloem," "thatch," and "plan." Appended

are a very selective glossary of the meaning of
botanical terms and a short bibliography.
7. Woodburn, Elisabeth. "Horticultural Heritage: The
Influence of U.S. Nurserymen." AGRICULTURE
LITERATURE: PROUD HERITAGE--FUTURE PROMISE, A
BICENTENNIAL SYMPOSIUM. Edited by Alan Fusonie,
and Leila Moran. Washington: Associates of the
National Agricultural Library/ Graduate School
Press, U.S.D.A., 1977. 109-141pp.
The bibliographic history of horticulture and
gardening in the United States was succinctly
treated by Elisabeth Woodburn, long one of the
most respected book dealers in the United States.
Major gardening books up to the mid-nineteenth
century are detailed in this thirty-page article.
A few black and white photographs from works
discussed are included. Appended is a chronology
of American horticultural works discussed in her
article.
8. Van Ravenswaay, Charles. A NINETEENTH-CENTURY GARDEN.
New York: Universe Books, 1977. 75p.
The history of the American nineteenth century
nursery trade is described in this short but
well-written book. Over 30 selected plates from
this period's nursery catalogues are excellently
reproduced. For each reproduction the text
explains gardening importance of the plant,
history of introduction, and use in the United
States. For instance, for Hovey's Seedling
Strawberry, "the great strawberry controversy" in
the 1840's is described, 54,000 bushels of
strawberries are listed as being sold in NYC in
1855, and Mr. Hovey's strawberry is stated to be
the first good strawberry to be introduced to
American gardens. This title serves as a good,
informal introduction to a little documented, yet
important aspect of U.S. horticultural history.
9. U.S. Dept. of Agriculture. YEARBOOK OF AGRICULTURE.
Washington, DC: Govt. Prt. Off., 1895-.
This annual compilation focuses on one broad topic
in agriculture or gardening each year. Many
times these annuals contain information pertinent
for gardeners. Among the yearbooks of recent
years are, GARDENING FOR FOOD AND FUN (1977), and
SEEDS (1961).
10. U.S. Superintendent of Documents. MONTHLY CATALOG OF
UNITED STATES GOVERNMENT PUBLICATIONS. Washington, DC:
Govt. Prt. Off., 1895-.

The following three titles are general reference
works that can access information on
government publications for gardeners. The MONTHLY
CATLAOG is a current listing of the publications
of all branches of the United States government.
Access is by author, title, subject,
series/report, contract number, stock number, and
title keyword. Many valuable titles published by
many agencies of government at a nominal cost are
of interest to gardeners.

11.  U.S. Superintendent to Documents. U.S. GOVERNMENT
     BOOKS. Washington, DC: Govt. Prt. Off., quarterly.
     A catalog listing of about 100 of the "most
     popular books, magazines, posters and maps"
     currently available. Published by the U.S.
     Government Printing Office, this title includes
     official order blanks and ordering information.
     Those wishing a copy of this catalog can request a
     free copy from Superintendent of Documents,
     Washington, DC 20402.

12.  AMERICAN STATISTICS INDEX. Washington, DC:
     Congressional Information Service, 1973-.
     An annual compilation published in two volumes
     which is "a comprehensive guide and index to
     the statistical publications of the U.S.
     Government." Volume one indexes subjects, names,
     categories, titles, and agency report numbers.
     The second volume contains abstracts by issuing
     agencies. ASI monthly supplements provide current
     month statistical abstracts and indexes which are
     superceded by the annual compilations.

13.  Hedrick, Ulysses Prentice. A HISTORY OF HORTICULTURE
     IN AMERICA TO 1860. New York: Oxford U. Press,
     1950. 551p.
     This title could be consulted for a reference to
     the history of horticulture in the United States.
     Its scope is limited and it does not include much
     recent research. There is a need for a newer,
     more comprehensive history of U.S. horticulture
     and gardening.


                 Botany and other Life Sciences


14.  INDEX KEWENSIS PLANTARUM PHANEROGAMARUM ....Oxford:
     Clarendon Press, 1893-95. 2 vol.

SUPPLEMENTUM....Oxford: Clarendon Press, 1901-.
[in progress] 16 vols-.
The official listing of genera and species of
flowering plants. It is arranged alphabetically
by genus. This index's coverage begins from the
time of Linneaus and with its supplements, it
covers recently discovered plants. The works in
which these genera were first published are listed
along with their naming authority and indication
of native country. Archaic names are also cross
referenced. Recent supplements cover subspecies
level information very selectively. Cultivars and
hybrids are ignored. A consolidated microform
edition is available. INDEX KEWENSIS is the
standard reference to check botanical names for
their correct nomenclature, naming authority,
family, and when they were first described.

15. FLOWERING PLANT INDEX OF ILLUSTRATION AND INFORMATION.
Compiled by Richard T. Isaacson. Boston: G.K.
Hall/The Garden Center of Greater Cleveland, 1979.
2 vols. 760,772p.
FLOWERING PLANT INDEX OF ILLUSTRATION AND INFORMATION,
1979-81. Boston: G.K. Hall/The Garden Center of
Greater Cleveland, 1982. 2 vols. 793,773p.
The four volumes of this flowering plant index
accesses over 100,000 entries arranged
alphabetically by botanical name. Each entry
leads one to an illustration of the plant and can
also lead to concomitant information on these
plants. Entries contain botanical name, author
and title of the indexed work, indication of
whether flower, fruit or habit is illustrated, and
the page/plate number on which the illustration
occurs. Also entries for common names are cross
referenced to botanical name. Works indexed are
generally post-1935 works found in the collections
of many libraries. A sampling of the index gives
access to 423 entries under Ranunculus, 71 under
Miltonia, and 235 under Oxalis. Common name cross
references would access 78 names under bean and
381 under orchid. Since its publication in 1982
this index is being automated to give more
detailed entries and also to facilitate
publication.

16. Willis, John Christopher. A DICTIONARY OF THE
FLOWERING PLANTS AND FERNS. 8th. ed. Revised by
H.K. Airy Shaw. Cambridge: University Press, 1973.
A dictionary listing genera of the world's

flowering plants and ferns. Correct genus name,
naming authority, and family are listed. Each
generic entry also indicates the approximate
number of species and where they are found
throughout the world. Detailed information on
families is also found. Archaic genera are listed
with cross references to correct names. (The last
edition seen by this reviewer is the 7th edition
of 1966).

17. INTERNATIONAL CODE OF BOTANICAL NOMENCLATURE ADOPTED
BY THE THIRTEENTH INTERNATIONAL BOTANICAL CONGRESS,
SYDNEY, AUGUST 1981. Utrecht: Bohn, Scheltema &
Holkema, 1983. Regnum vegetabile, vol III. 472p.
The last revision of these rules for the naming of
plants should be consulted whenever any questions
on nomenclature arise. The naming, ranking,
effective and valid publication, and orthography
of names are defined. These rules are given in
English, French, and German.

18. Gray, Asa. GRAY'S MANUAL OF BOTANY; A HANDBOOK OF THE
FLOWERING PLANTS AND FERNS OF THE CENTRAL AND
NORTHEASTERN UNITED STATES AND ADJACENT CANADA.
8th. ed. Largely rewritten and expanded by Merritt
Lyndon Fernald. New York: American Book, 1950.
1632p.
Arranged by family, 8,340 vascular plants are
described with habitat, and range. Family,
genera, species, and subspecies information is
listed. Family keys for identification purposes
are included. Appended are a glossary and
separate indexes for botanical and common names.
This is a standard botanical reference especially
useful for identifying native North American
plants, otherwise it is of limited value to most
gardeners.

19. BIOLOGICAL & AGRICULTURAL INDEX. New York: Wilson,
1964-.
Superseding AGRICULTURAL INDEX (1916-64), this
index gives limited coverage to periodicals of
interest to gardeners. Most popular gardening
magazines, publications of plant societies, and
horticultural societies are not indexed in this
title.

20. AGRICOLA. Beltsville, MD: National Agricultural
Library, 1970-.
This database could access information on many
subjects of interest to gardeners. It contains
comprehensive coverage of worldwide journal and

monographic literature on agriculture and many
related disciplines. About 2,000,000 entries were
included as of 1984. AGRICOLA is divided into two
files, one accessing records of the period 1970-
78, and the other 1979 to date. This database is
available through on-line database vendors.

21. INDEX LONDINENSIS TO FLOWERING PLANTS, FERNS AND
FERN ALLIES....Oxford: Clarendon Press, 1929-31.
6 vols.
SUPPLEMENT FOR THE YEARS 1921-35....Oxford:
Clarendon Press, 1941. 2 vols.
Arranged alphabetically by genera, INDEX
LONDINENSIS is used to find illustrations of
flowering plants and ferns in published works
prior to 1935. It is a monumental work. For
post-1935 illustrated works, THE FLOWERING PLANT
INDEX (15), can be consulted.

22. Smith, Roger C.; W. Malcolm Reid; and Arlene E.
Luchsinger. SMITH'S GUIDE TO THE LITERATURE OF THE
LIFE SCIENCES. 9th. ed. Minneapolis: Burgess
Pub., 1980. 223p.
Research methods are defined, libraries and their
classification methods are explored, and many
reference titles are defined in this broad title
on the life sciences. Taxonomies for these
disciplines are also introduced. Scientific
writing, theses, and dissertations are also
discussed. Reasonably up-to-date, this guide
could be a useful reference source for those
researching gardening and related fields.

23. Swift, Lloyd H. BOTANICAL BIBLIOGRAPHIES; A GUIDE TO
BIBLIOGRAPHIC MATERIALS APPLICABLE TO BOTANY.
Minneapolis: Burgess, 1970. 804p.
As a guide to the literature of botany, this title
could be used by a researcher. Index of
authors, subjects, and titles.

24. Cronquist, Arthur. BASIC BOTANY. New York: Harper &
Row, 1981.
The science of botany with its structure,
taxonomy, plant structure, processes, evolution,
heredity, plant communities, and plant geography
is introduced in this basic botany textbook. There
are many other competing books on begining botany,
but this is one of the best.

25. Glimn-Lacy, Janice, and Peter B. Kaufman. BOTANY
ILLUSTRATED: INTRODUCTION TO PLANTS, MAJOR GROUPS,
FLOWERING PLANT FAMILIES. New York: Van Nostrand

Reinhold, 1984. 146p.
For a simplified introduction to the science of
botany, amateurs might want to refer to this
title. Plant structure and processes and plant
taxonomy are briefly introduced. Major groups and
selected flowering plant families are defined.
The many drawings are a feature of this elementary
text.

26. Stearn, William T. BOTANICAL LATIN: HISTORY, GRAMMAR,
SYNTAX, TERMINOLOGY, AND VOLCABULARY. 3rd ed., rev.
North Pomfret, VT: David & Charles, 1983.
The grammar and syntax of botanical terms are
defined in depth in this impressive work. A 150-
page vocabulary of terms that describe plants
provides both Latin-English and English-Latin
equivalents. A short history of the development
of botanical terminology is found in the
introduction.

27. Hardin, James Walker, and Jay M. Arena. HUMAN
POISONING FROM NATIVE AND CULTIVATED PLANTS.
2d. ed. Durham, NC: Duke University Press,
1974. 194p.
While other texts provide more technical and
inclusive information on poisonous plants, this
text gives sane advice on most plants that should
be regarded as toxic. Arranged mainly by family,
the genera (with common names) that have toxic
principles are listed. For each major plant,
description, occurrence and poisoning principles
are listed. It is well illustrated with both
drawings and photographs.

28. Little, R. John, and C. Eugene Jones. A DICTIONARY
OF BOTANY. New York: Van Nostrand Reinhold, 1980.
400p.
For botanical terminology, this title has "nearly
5,500" definitions. The definitions are concise
and avoid technical jargon. There are some
drawings. There are more complete botanical
dictionaries (29), but this title would be useful
for the amateur.

29. ELSEVIER'S DICTIONARY OF BOTANY: IN ENGLISH, FRENCH,
GERMAN, LATIN, AND RUSSIAN. Compiled by Paul Macura.
New York: Elsevier Scientific Pub., 1979- 2 vols.
For those seeking common names of a large number
of the world's plants in major European languages,
volume one of this dictionary could be of use. In
one basic table, equivalent names in English,
French, German and Latin can be found. Russian
equivalents are listed separately. Volume two

lists general botanical terms.
30. Schery, Robert W. PLANTS FOR MAN. 2nd ed.
    Englewood Cliffs, NJ: Prentice-Hall, 1972. 657p.
    The broad subject of man's relationship with and
    economic    interest in plants is introduced in
    this fact-filled text. Economic plants from
    throughout the world are briefly defined in
    nontechnical terminology. Statistics, descrip-
    tions, black and white photographs, historical
    information, and economic importance of each crop
    or plants are included. The arrangement is by
    such broad subject chapters such as fruits,
    beverage plants, cereals, etc. All chapters have
    suggested supplemental reading.
31. Martin, Alexander Campbell, and William D. Barkely.
    SEED IDENTIFICATION MANUAL. Berkeley, CA:
    University of California Press, 1961. 221p.
    Oriented towards seeds that are of interest to
    agriculturalists, foresters, and wildlife
    biologists, this identification manual might be of
    interest to gardeners looking for illustrations of
    wild plant seeds. Photographs and drawings of
    more than 600 seeds are included. Also included
    are identification characteristics of major plant
    families. Gardeners will not find many of the
    ornamental perennial or annual seeds or vegetable
    seeds pictured here. Other sources of
    illustrations of seeds include SEEDS OF WOODY
    PLANTS IN THE UNITED STATES (467), and Symonds
    identification manuals for trees (259) and shrubs
    (274).
32. Miller, Orson K, Jr. MUSHROOMS OF NORTH AMERICA.
    New York: Dutton, 1972. 359p.
    Those needing help in identifying mushrooms will
    appreciate the 292 color photographs in this
    identification manual. Also included are chapters
    on collecting and preparing mushrooms for eating.
    A sane discussion of mushrooms with toxic
    principles is included.
33. Hunt, Rachel McMasters Miller. CATALOGUE OF BOTANICAL
    BOOKS IN THE COLLECTION OF RACHEL McMASTERS MILLER
    HUNT. Compiled by Jane Quinby. Pittsburgh: Hunt
    Botanical Library, 1958-61. v.1-2 in 3.
    ccxliv,517,665p.
    A catalogue of a small portion of the collection
    of The Hunt Botanical Library, now part of the
    Hunt Institute for Botanical Documentation.
    Coverage is of books published prior to 1800.

Entries contain detailed bibilographic descriptions, collations, with annotations giving
historical importance. Detailed indexes are
included. This catalogue would be an excellent
source for those looking for detailed information
on the more valuable pre-1800 gardening and
botanical titles.

34.  Blunt, Wilfrid. THE ART OF BOTANICAL ILLUSTRATION.
     London: Collins, 1950. 304p.
     A well illustrated, historical account of the
     development of the art of botanical
     illustration from its beginnings into the
     twentieth century. In this transversal most of
     the famous botanical artists and important
     illustrated works in botany and horticulture are
     covered. While it is a scholarly book,
     nonspecialists will enjoy this classic study.

35.  Ayensu, Edward S., and Robert A. DeFilipps.
     ENDANGERED AND THREATENED PLANTS OF THE UNITED
     STATES. Washington: Smithsonian Institution,
     1978. 403p.
     This comprehensive although somewhat out-of-date
     manual details many of the plants that are
     endangered or threatened in the United States.
     Approximately 10% of the vascular flora of the
     United States and 50% of the Hawaiian flora are so
     listed. Preliminary chapters discuss factors
     which have caused these plants to be threatened.
     Conservation methods are discussed. A
     bibliography of state publications (as of 1978) is
     included. It is partially out of date because of
     the tremendous amount of publication in this field
     since 1978.

36.  Simonds, John Ormsbee. EARTHSCAPE: A MANUAL OF
     ENVIRONMENTAL PLANNING. New York: McGraw-Hill,
     1978. 339p.
     A wide-ranging manual on environmental planning
     focusing on land, air, and water resources with
     their concomitant pollution problems. Regional
     planning and conservation methods are introduced.
     Excellently designed and illustrated.


                    Gardening Encyclopedias


37.  Bailey, L.H. HORTUS THIRD: A CONCISE DICTIONARY OF

PLANTS CULTIVATED IN THE UNITED STATES AND CANADA.
Initially compiled by L.H. Bailey and Ethel Zoe
Bailey; revised and expanded by the staff of the
Liberty Hyde Bailey Hortorium.  New York:
Macmillan, 1976.  1290p.
HORTUS THIRD is the most often cited reference
work in horticulture or gardening.  It accurately
names and describes 281 families, 3,301 genera,
20,397 species, and many more subspecies,
varieties, forms and cultivars of plants of
horticultural importance.  The included plants are
those that the compilers from the Bailey Hortorium
at Cornell University cite as being generally
cultivated in North American horticulture.
Arranged alphabetically by genus, each generic
entry includes indication of family, cultivated
speces, naming authorities, detailed botanical
descriptions and very limited cultural
information.  There are entries also on
horticulturally important plant families and some
general articles (cacti and succulents, hotbeds,
forcing, lawns, etc.).  The few drawings are
limited to family entries.  Appended are lists of
naming authority abbreviations, a detailed
glossary of botanical terms, and a very
comprehensive common name index.  This is the most
up-to-date and complete reference to cultivated
plants.  HORTUS THIRD should be consulted whenever
questions on nomenclature or descriptions of
horticultural plants arise.

38.    Everett, Thomas H.  THE NEW YORK BOTANICAL GARDEN
ILLUSTRATED ENCYCLOPEDIA OF HORTICULTURE.
New York: Garland Pub., 1980-82.  10 vols.  3601p.
The ten volumes of this landmark encyclopedia
cover 3,600 genera and contain over 10,000
photographs and in excess of 3,000,000 words.
While these statistics are impressive, it is
through daily use that one finds the true value of
this work.  Along with the alphabetical generic
entries are found many other entries on plant
families, garden terms and processes, plant
anatomy and terms, types of gardens and gardening,
and plant problems.  Cross references from common
names are extensively given.  The detail of the
generic entries is impressive.  Pronunciations,

common names, family, habitat, and the most
commonly cultivated species are included.
Descriptions are given in a clear nontechnical
manner. Garden and landscape use of the plants
included are emphasized. Cultivation advice is
concise and seems to be written by someone who has
growing knowledge of each plant. Information is
included on the cultivation of thousands of the
world's plants in greater depth than in many
specific cultural manuals. This encyclopedia is
also balanced in that it, for instance, does not
favor woody plants over greenhouse plants or treat
perennials in greater detail than vegetables as do
many other horticultural encyclopedias. The black
and white and color photography is excellent and
always pertinent, not just decorative as one finds
in other encyclopedias. Mr. Everett's prose is
constantly fresh and exact. It allows one to
picture the plant as he describes them (for
instance, "it has twice-divided leaves, those on
the stem diminishing in size above," or, "These
plants have erect stems, alternate leaves, and
solitary daisylike heads with yellow centers and
white, blue, purple, or violet rays. The fruits
are achenes.") Because of the detail in this work
it sometimes is necessary to read long entries to
find specific information. American gardeners are
supremely fortunate to have a work of this
magnitude and depth to consult. This encyclopedia
and HORTUS THIRD (37), are probably the most
consulted works in gardening literature.

39. Wyman, Donald. WYMAN'S GARDENING ENCYCLOPEDIA.
Rev. ed. New York: Macmillan, 1977. 1221p.
The best one-volume gardening encyclopedia. Dr.
Wyman is one of America's most respected
plantsmen and his encyclopedia exhibits much
first-hand knowledge. Arranged alphabetically by
genera it concisely describes many of the genera,
species and cultivars cultivated in North America.
Unique in gardening encyclopedias is its listing
of plant hardiness using the Arnold Arboretum
hardiness zone map of the United States and
Canada. Hardiness indications are difficult to
find elsewhere. Careful plant descriptions,
pronunciations of generic names, and habitat
information are also given. Garden terms and

processes, and plant parts are included and
clearly defined. Cross references from common
names are included. This handy one volume
encyclopedia will, one hopes, be periodically
updated for future generations of American
gardeners.

40. Bailey, L.H. MANUAL OF CULTIVATED PLANTS MOST
    COMMONLY GROWN IN THE UNITED STATES AND CANADA.
    Rev. ed. New York: Macmillan, 1957. 1116p.
    This manual although out of date remains useful as
    it provides     access to commonly grown plants   by
    family. The     revised   edition  includes   194
    families, 15,532 genera and 5,347 species. Naming
    authority, botanical description, some drawings,
    and  indication  of native habitat are  given  for
    most entries. Family and some selective genus and
    species identification keys are included.   An 86-
    page index references genera with species, common
    names, and incidentally mentioned plants.

41. Graf, Alfred Byrd. EXOTICA, SERIES 4: PICTORIAL
    CYCYLOPEDIA OF EXOTIC PLANTS FROM TROPICAL AND
    NEAR-TROPIC REGIONS. East Rutherford, NJ: Roehrs,
    1982.
    Similiar in treatment to the EXOTIC PLANT MANUAL
    (42), this book features much larger photographs
    and contains 16,300 photographs (as opposed to
    4,200) of tropical plants. This pictorial
    encyclopedia is arranged alphabetically by family
    so it is easy to identify plants once family
    characteristics are recognized. Cultural
    information is found in keyed form (indications of
    water, light, and temperature requirements) in the
    separate encyclopedic section of text. This title
    is more useful than the EXOTIC PLANT MANUAL as
    there are more plants included and the photographs
    are clearer and larger.

42. Graf, Alfred Byrd. EXOTIC PLANT MANUAL: FASCINATING
    PLANTS TO LIVE WITH--THEIR REQUIREMENTS,
    PROPAGATION, AND USE. 4th ed. East Rutherford,
    NJ: Roehrs, 1976. 840p.
    Arranged by broad plant types (cacti, bromeliads,
    vines, ferns), this manual includes 4,200 small
    black and white photographs of tropical and
    subtropical plants of the world. The manual is
    particularly useful as a pictorial identification
    manual of plants commonly grown indoors in the

North. A separate encyclopedic section of text arranged by genus describes the pictured plants. Pictograph symbols are used on each photograph to indicate cultural requirements. Botanical and common names are listed below the photographs. A general section gives houseplant cultural advice while other sections discuss decorating with plants and tropical plant geography. There are separate common name and generic indexes. See also entries for EXOTICA 4 (41) and TROPICA (43).

43. Graf, Alfred Byrd. TROPICA: COLOR CYCLOPEDIA OF EXOTIC PLANTS AND TREES FOR WARM REGION HORTICULTURE--IN COOL CLIMATE, THE SUMMER GARDEN OR SHELTERED INDOORS. 2d. ed., rev. and enl. East Rutherford, NJ: Roehrs, 1978. 1120p.

This pictorial encyclopedia contains over 7,000 color photographs and is similiar in treatment to EXOTICA (41). In the text the generic listings are given cultural advice in short key word form (such as warm-temperate, subtropic). Appended are a common name index, a generic index, and a short entry bibliography. The color photographs are of variable quality.

44. THE ROYAL HORTICULTURAL SOCIETY DICTIONARY OF GARDENING: A PRACTICAL AND SCIENTIFIC ENCYCLOPEDIA OF HORTICULTURE. Ed. by Fred J. Chittenden. Oxford: Clarendon Press, 1951. 4 vols. 2316p. THE ROYAL HORTICULTURAL SOCIETY SUPPLEMENT TO THE DICTIONARY OF GARDENING...Ed. by Patrick M. Synge. Oxford: Clarendon Press, 1956. 1 vol. 334p.

A useful encyclopedia especially for its emphasis on plants commonly grown in England and for its discussions of English growing methods. Arranged alphabetically by genera, each listing describes for whom each genera was named, family, cultivated species, and descriptive, historical, and cultural information. Species entries include short botanical descriptions, indicate native habitats, and when the species were discovered. Most of the work was done on this encyclopedia in the late 1930's and 1940's and the entries are signed by their contributors. The supplement lists important pre-1956 cultivars and hybrids along with additions and corrections for the first 4 volumes.

45. Bailey, L.H. THE STANDARD CYCLOPEDIA OF HORTICULTURE.

2d. ed. New York: Macmillan, 1941. 3 vols. 3639p.
First published in 1900, this popular gardening
encyclopedia has gone through many printings.
Although certainly superseded by newer
encyclopedias, it is still consulted for its
historical importance, its clear drawings, and for
some of its cultural information. It originally
was published in six volumes and contained some
material that was not included in the three-volume
editions (including a useful section on 19th
century American horticulturists).

46. THE TIME-LIFE ENCYCLOPEDIA OF GARDENING. Alexandria,
    VA: Time-Life, 1971-79.
    This multi-volume encyclopedia has been deservedly
    popular. Each volume is usually on a different
    gardening topic, and many of them are found in
    this bibliography (see index). Generally they are
    well illustrated with both photographs and
    drawings and feature concise information. Most
    have encyclopedic sections of plants pertinent to
    each volume's subject. An index was published
    covering only the first number of volumes in this
    series.

47. Hay, Roy, and Patrick M. Synge. THE COLOR DICTIONARY
    OF FLOWERS AND PLANTS FOR HOME AND GARDEN.
    New York: Crown Pub., 1969. 373p.
    Over 2,000 small color photographs of cultivated
    trees, shrubs, perennials, annuals, bulbs, and
    greenhouse plants are included in this English
    title. For each plant a descriptive listing is
    also included giving ornamental use and blooming
    time. Since this title has such a wide coverage of
    ornamental plants, it is useful to novice
    gardeners for identification purposes.

48. Perry, Frances, and Leslie Greenwood, illus. FLOWERS
    OF THE WORLD. New York: Bonanza, 1981. 320p.
    828 beautiful colored paintings by Leslie
    Greenwood of a selection of the more commonly
    grown flowering plants of the world is the feature
    of this title. Arranged by family, the text
    indicates for each how many genera and species are
    found, where they are native, and gives short
    descriptions of many genera and species.

49. READER'S DIGEST ENCYCLOPAEDIA OF GARDEN PLANTS AND
    FLOWERS. Edited by Roy Hay. New York: Reader's
    Digest Association, 1978. 799p.
    Descriptions of over 3,000 cultivated plants with

over 2,000    small color photographs are featured
in this encyclopedia written in England.   Cultural
information,      native      habitat,      description,
propagation,   and possible pests and diseases   are
given   in   concise   form.    This   title   is   again
arranged   by   genera.    The   photographs   are   of
variable quality.

50.  American Horticultural Society.  AMERICAN HORTICULTURAL
     SOCIETY ILLUSTRATED ENCYCLOPEDIA OF GARDENING.
     Mount Vernon, VA: author, 1982–84.
     Of  less value than the TIME–LIFE ENCYCLOPEDIA  OF
     GARDENING  (46)  but similar in subject  treatment
     and format.   Most of the information was compiled
     by the staff of Ortho Publications.   Each  volume
     is popularly written and colorfully illustrated.

51.  Wright, Michael.   THE COMPLETE HANDBOOK OF GARDEN
     PLANTS.  New York:  Facts on File, 1984.  544p.
     Over  2,500 very small,  variable quality  colored
     drawings of      garden plants are the feature  of
     this manual.   The text is divided into chapters on
     trees,   shrubs,  vines, perennials, annuals, bulbs,
     rock  plants,   and  water  plants.   Included  is
     information on 9,000 species and varieties so   the
     text  is  necessarily very brief.   This title  is
     useful only for very brief information but it does
     include an amazing number of plants.   Best used in
     conjunction with more detailed titles.

52.  Ferguson, Nicola.  RIGHT PLANT, RIGHT PLACE.
     Edited by Fred McGourty.  New York: Summit Books,
     1984.  292p.
     An English title that is useful in helping to make
     plant      selections for many different  gardening
     situations.   Over  25  different  categories  are
     included some of which are:  plants for heavy clay
     soils,   for   dry shade,   for   hedging,   with  grey
     leaves,  with fragrant flowers and more.   For each
     category,  small color photographs are featured of
     the  selected plants along with brief  information
     listing  flowering season,  flower color,  height,
     and  a  description of how the  plants  are  used.
     Many    symbols    and    abbreviations    are    used
     throughout.   Lists  of  alternative  plants   to
     consider  are  included.   It has  been  partially
     edited for North American conditions.

53.  Perry, Frances, and Roy Hay.  A FIELD GUIDE TO
     TROPICAL AND SUBTROPICAL PLANTS.  New York:

Van Nostrand Reinhold, 1982. 136p.
Almost 200 trees, shrubs, vines, and water plants
of the tropics    and subtropics are identified in
this small title.    Three or four color phtographs
are included per page with accompanying text
giving family, genus, and species with common
name, place of origin, a nontechnical description,
blooming season, and how grown. A very selective
identification guide.

54.  Elliot, W. Rodger, and David L. Jones. ENCYCLOPAEDIA
OF AUSTRALIAN PLANTS SUITABLE FOR CULTIVATION.
Melbourne: Lothian Pub., 1980-. In progress,
to be published in 4 volumes.
This four-volume encyclopedia is, of course,
valuable as a source of information on Australian
gardening and plants but also is pertinent to the
areas of the United States (such as parts of the
United States Southwest) that have similar
climatic conditions. Volume 1 introduces
gardening practices in Australia while volume 2
starts the encyclopedic entries listed by genera.
The preface to volume 2 states "our aim has been
to include all species of Australian plants that
have been cultivated." Entries are brief but
contain much practical information of interest to
gardeners. There are many drawings and color
photographs.

55.  NEW ILLUSTRATED ENCYCLOPEDIA OF GARDENING, UNABRIDGED.
Edited by T.H. Everett. New York: Greystone
Press, 1960. 17 vols.
While still of value, this encyclopedia has
certainly been superseded by Mr. Everett's new
encyclopedia (38). Published in 14 volumes with 3
supplementary subject volumes, it was for many
years one of the most useful reference works. Mr.
Everett's new encyclopedia is not only up-to-date
but is also more inclusive. His new work was also
entirely written by himself.


## Gardening Manuals


*  Everett, Thomas H. THE NEW YORK BOTANICAL GARDEN
ILLUSTRATED ENCYCLOPEDIA OF HORTICULTURE. Cited
above as item 38.
See main review. This encyclopedia needs to be
mentioned again    because of its extensive

practical gardening information. It gives
detailed discussions on how to grow gardening
plants as well as being gardening's most inclusive
encyclopedia.

56.  Bush-Brown, James, and Louise Bush-Brown. AMERICA'S
     GARDEN BOOK. Rev. ed. by The New York Botanical
     Garden. New York: Scribner, 1980. 819p.
     First published in 1939 and revised periodically,
     this title has been America's most popular
     gardening manual. It is so often consulted
     because it is one of the most inclusive of one
     volume gardening manuals and contains very
     practical information. This manual is divided
     into broad sections on garden design, the
     selection and care of landscape plants (lawns,
     trees, shrubs, perennials, etc.), vegetable, fruit
     and herb growing, indoor gardening, and cultural
     methods. As necessary in this type of manual
     there is a lot of detail, but the many
     illustrations and tables help present this
     material in an understandable format. The depth
     of coverage is outstanding. For instance, on iris
     a good selection of species, cultivars, and
     hybrids are described, growing irises are defined
     in detail, diseases and pests are listed along
     with control measures, while other information
     includes a short history of irises, and the
     address of the American Iris Society. This amount
     of detailed information is found for many
     gardening subjects. Appended are addresses of
     major plant societies, a very short glossary, and
     a hardiness zone map. A good index is included.
     A gardener will not find everything on practical
     gardening he/she is seeking, but it is the one-
     volume source to consult first.

57.  Abraham, George, and Katy Abraham. THE GREEN THUMB
     GARDEN HANDBOOK. Rev ed. Englewood Cliffs, NJ:
     Prentice-Hall, 1977. 528p.
     The emphasis of this gardening manual is practical
     advice. It was written by two of America's
     most experienced gardeners and garden writers.
     Whether one looks for answers to what types of
     grass for lawns, how to control iris borers, how
     to water houseplants, when to spray fruit trees,

or how to care for herbs, one finds good practical advice. It is a very good quick reference, and one of the best one volume gardening manuals. There are few illustrations but they are not missed as the information is comprehensive and accurately presented.

58.  READER'S DIGEST ILLUSTRATED GUIDE TO GARDENING.
Edited by Caroll C. Calkins. Pleasantville, NY: Reader's Digest Association, 1978. 672p.
Another very detailed one volume garden manual. Here the many illustrations are the most valuable feature. The drawings especially are helpful as they show how to prune, to double dig a garden, to take softwood cuttings, and much more. The text is divided into broad sections such as gardening outdoors (lawns to trees), growing food plants, and indoor gardening. Landscape design basics are not well covered. Not as inclusive as Bush-Brown (56), although it still contains a surprising amount of information.

59.  Johnson, Hugh. THE PRINCIPLES OF GARDENING: A GUIDE TO THE ART, HISTORY, SCIENCE AND PRACTICE OF GARDENING. New York: Simon & Schuster, 1979. 272p.
A large, glossy gardening manual that features color photographs of gardens and gardening plants. It does have merit, especially in the good chapters on plant material (roses, rhododendrons, bulbs, perennials). Also Mr. Johnson's advice on garden planning would be useful. It would be best used in conjunction with other more practical garden manuals. An English title.

60.  THE WISLEY BOOK OF GARDENING: A GUIDE FOR ENTHUSIASTS.
Edited by Robert Pearson. New York: Norton, 1983. 352p.
Since English gardening books are so popular in this country, perhaps this title edited at The Royal Horticultural Society's Wisley Garden will help North American gardeners translate some of England's unfamiliar gardening terminology and practices. Each section is written by a recognized English authority. For instance, the chapter on alpine houses is written by Will Ingwersen, shrubs by Roy Lancaster, and herbaceous perennials by Graham Stuart Thomas. Experienced gardeners will find a lot of useful information; novice gardeners should look to manuals more

oriented to North American gardening conditions.

61.   Wilson, Lois. THE COMPLETE GARDENER; A LIVELY
      PRACTICAL GUIDE WHEREVER YOU LIVE. New York:
      Hawthorn Books, 1972. 431p.
      Although somewhat out of date, this general
      gardening manual is still useful. Attractively
      arranged, it leads the gardener through beginning
      garden construction, describes many basic
      gardening tasks (digging, transplanting, etc.),
      discusses plant selection (from trees to annuals),
      and introduces indoor gardening. Short guides to
      gardening in eleven climatic regions of the United
      States are appended.

62.   10,000 GARDEN QUESTIONS ANSWERED BY 20 EXPERTS.
      Ed. by Marjorie J. Dietz. 4th. ed. Garden City,
      NY: Doubleday, 1982. 1507p.
      Forty years of being in print must indicate that
      this title has been useful to gardeners. This
      fourth edition has been updated and could answer
      many gardening questions. Arrangement is by broad
      subject matter such as roses, lawns and turf
      areas, houseplants, etc. Best used as a reference
      as most will find the question and answer format
      irritating to use at length.

63.   Wallach, Carla. GARDENING IN THE CITY: BACKYARDS,
      BALCONIES, TERRACES AND PENTHOUSES. New York:
      Harcourt Brace Jovanovich, 1976. 176p.
      This New York City garden writer has produced a
      focused title on the challenge of gardening in
      an urban area. Backyard, balcony, terrace, and
      penthouse gardening are defined and evaluated for
      their gardening possibilities and challenges.
      Diverse information on planning and maintaining
      these areas is presented even to composting and
      vegetable gardening on a small scale. While
      certainly not as detailed as most general
      gardening manuals, this title does answer basic
      questions for those establishing gardens in these
      conditions. See also container gardening (130).

64.   James, John. FLOWERS WHEN YOU WANT THEM: A GROWER'S
      GUIDE TO OUT-OF-SEASON BLOOM. New York: Hawthorn
      Books, 1977. 267p.
      Forcing bulbs, pot plants, tree and shrub
      branches, and cut flowers indoors and in the
      greenhouse are well covered in this unique title.
      Specifics of forcing, and tables giving

seeding/forcing schedules are included. For instance, details on forcing snapdragons include which varieties force well and at what time seed should be sowed and plants started. Appended are a general yearly schedule, a metric conversion table, and a short glossary. This information is difficult to find elsewhere other than in technical horticultural manuals.

65. Hamblin, Stephen Francis. LISTS OF PLANT TYPES FOR LANDSCAPE PLANTING; THE MATERIALS OF PLANTING FOR ORNAMENT LISTED ACCORDING TO THEIR VARIOUS USES. Cambridge: Harvard University Press, 1929. 163p.
This title is still valuable as a plant selection tool as it consists of lists giving growing heights, rate of growth, use, flower color, season of bloom, soil preferences and much more for many ornamental plants. Among the plants treated are trees, shrubs, vines, perennials, and annuals. Gardeners would find the 163 pages of lists in this text of great help when planning their gardens and landscapes.

66. Rose, Graham. THE LOW MAINTENANCE GARDEN. New York: Viking Press, 1983. 168p.
Written in England, this title has been edited for North American conditions by the New York Botanical Garden Institute of Urban Horticulture. It features plans for many different types of small gardens for urban landscapes. Low maintenance features include incorporating paving materials in the landscape, using minimum care plants, water gardens, irrigation, mulches, raised beds and much more. Practical plans with recommended plant material and construction materials are included. Planning is emphasized over planting and upkeep. Attractively illustrated.

67. Taloumis, George. WINTERIZE YOUR YARD AND GARDEN. Philadelphia, Lippincott, 1976. 288p.
Covering the seasons fall through spring, much practical advice is given on plant care and landscape maintenance. Fall to winter care of evergreens, roses, lawns and fruit trees is covered, followed with garden chores that can be done in the winter. Finally, spring clean up and preparatory care of landscape plants is introduced. A discussion covering the same time

period   for   gardening   in   the   South   is   also
included.  Good practical advice for gardeners.

68.   PRACTICAL GARDENING ENCYCLOPEDIA.  Edited by Roy Hay
and George Elbert.  New York: Van Nostrand
Reinhold, 1977.  351p.
This gardening manual is more limited in  coverage
and certainly    lacks the detail of other manuals
(much less detail on specific plants,  on diseases
and   pests with control measures,  etc.)  Produced
in  England  and  partially  edited  for  American
growing  conditions,  gardeners  could  find  some
useful  information  here,  but  this  text  lacks
detail.

### Regional Gardening Manuals

(These   manuals   can be among the   most   important
reference  books  for  gardeners.  Listed  are  a
selection of those the compiler has found.   There
are   probably   many   other   excellent   regional
gardening guides.  See also the regional gardening
titles  on  using  native  plants,  woody  plants,
regional periodicals, etc.)

### NORTHEASTERN UNITED STATES

(Most  of  the  general  gardening  manuals  listed
above,  (56-68)  were written with  this  region's
gardening conditions in mind).

### SOUTHERN UNITED STATES

69.   SOUTHERN LIVING GARDEN GUIDE: HOUSEPLANTS, VEGETABLES,
TREES, SHRUBS AND MORE.  Birmingham, AL:  Oxmoor
House, 1981.  224p.
Oxmoor  House  publishes excellent guides for  the
South including    this general gardening  manual,
one   on   woody   plants   (247),   and   another   on
vegetable   gardening   (313).   They   are   all
handsomely produced with excellent  illustrations.
This  title follows a question-and-answer  format,
posing   general  gardening  questions  and   then
providing concise answers.   There are chapters on
wildflowers,   bulbs,   annuals and perennials,   and
trees  and  shrubs.   It is a selective guide  and
certainly will not answer all gardening questions.
This  manual's climatic region is not defined  but
seems  to  be  designed  for  the  Southern  region

excluding subtropical Florida.
70. Noble, Mary. GARDEN IN FLORIDA: MONTHLY TIMETABLES
AND PLANTING GUIDES. Rev. ed. Jacksonville, FL:
author, 1975.
This handy paperback answers many questions about
gardening in the different climatic regions of
Florida. There is much gardening information
given, with planting guides and useful monthly
timetables. Originally published as YOU CAN
GARDEN IN FLORIDA.

NORTHERN UNITED STATES

71. Snyder, Leon C. GARDENING IN THE UPPER MIDWEST.
Minneapolis: University of Minnesota Press, 1978.
292p.
Dr. Snyder is director emeritus of the University
of Minnesota Landscape Arboretum and was for
many years head of the University's department of
horticulture. This manual is an excellent
introduction to gardening in the North. More
detailed than many regional manuals, the author
discusses in depth soil preparation, lawns, fruit,
and the selection and care of landscape and
gardening plants. Information is given concisely
with many lists of plants for specific purposes.
First hand growing experience is evidenced in this
title, as in his titles on woody plants (245) and
garden flowers (154). All are indispensable for
this climatic region.
72. Hill, Lewis. SUCCESSFUL COLD-CLIMATE GARDENING.
Brattleboro, VT: Stephen Greene Press, 1981. 308p.
Spring and fall frost injury, extremely cold
temperatures, sunscald, snow and ice damage are
among the "challenges" Mr. Hill cites for
gardeners in the North. Practical, brief advice
is given for the selection and care of vegetables,
fruit, nuts, trees, shrubs, perennials, ground
covers, vines and lawns in these climatic
conditions. Gardeners would need to consult other
gardening titles to supplement the advice found
here. It does contain a lot of helpful
information for the novice Northern gardener.

ROCKY MOUNTAIN STATES

73. Gundell, Herb. HERB GUNDELL'S COMPLETE GUIDE TO

ROCKY MOUNTAIN GARDENING. Dallas: Taylor Pub.,
1985. 407p.
The difficult climatic extremes in this region
require that gardeners use different growing
techniques. This up-to-date and well organized
gardening manual gives many specific cultural tips
for growing plants in this region. The author
states, "We cannot depend very much on the
weather, on the seasons or on the soils of the
Rocky Mountain territory..." Landscaping, lawns,
ornamentals and much more are included. The
SUNSET NEW WESTERN GARDEN BOOK (74) also covers
this gardening region.

## WESTERN UNITED STATES

74.  SUNSET NEW WESTERN GARDEN BOOK. By the editor of
     Sunset Books and Sunset Magazine. 4th. ed.
     Menlo Park, CA: Lane Pub., 1979. 512p.
     Gardening in the diverse climatic conditions of
     the Western U.S. (from Montana-New Mexico
     westward) is well covered in this excellently
     produced gardening manual. 24 (!) climatic
     regions are defined considering such factors as
     temperature, rainfall, elevation, and terrain.
     About three-fourths of this manual consists of a
     "Western plant encyclopedia" of 6,000 plants.
     These plants are arranged alphabetically by genus
     with cross references from common names. Each
     plant is non-technically described with landscape
     use and hardiness indication included. Small
     sketches give identification characteristics. A
     section on plant selection defines which plants
     should be considered for different garden and
     landscape purposes, from plants for rock gardens
     to those that are fire retardant. Basic gardening
     and plant care is discussed in concise form in
     other sections of this manual. Western gardeners
     will consult this title often. The publisher
     updates this quality publication regularly.

## NORTHWESTERN UNITED STATES

(The SUNSET NEW WESTERN GARDEN BOOK (74) covers
this region as do the following more specific
titles: McNeilan on vegetables and fruits (314),
and Kruckeberg (127) on using native plants.)

CANADA
(Canada has almost as wide ranging climatic
regions as found in the United States. Some of
the regional gardening manuals from contiguous
United States states might be of interest to
Canadian gardeners. See also the specific titles
on woody plants, vegetable gardening, and
periodicals written specifically for Canadian
gardeners.)

* Wilson, Lois. THE COMPLETE GARDENER. Cited above as
   item 61.
   Although written by a Canadian writer, this title
   is of no more value to Canadians than other
   general gardening manuals. This author has
   written a manual titled: CHATELAINE'S GARDENING
   BOOK published by Doubleday Canada which this
   compiler has not seen.

75. Perron, W.H. ENCYCLOPEDIE DU JARDINIER HORTICULEUR;
   EMBELLISSONS NOS DEMEURES EN APPROFONDISSANT NOS
   CONNAISSANCES EN HORTICULTURE. Montreal:
   Le Editions de L'Homme, 1971. 415p.
   For French Canadians this older title would be
   useful. This manual covers vegetables, fruit,
   flower gardening, and landscape plant materials.
   Cultivars and hybrids recommended are out-of-date.
   Also garden preparation and garden practices are
   too briefly covered. It was written specifically
   for Quebec and the St. Lawrence valley but would
   be of interest to anyone seeking information on
   general gardening in French.


Organic Gardening
(see also books on soils (473-74) and the
periodicals (530) listed.)

76. THE ENCYCLOPEDIA OF ORGANIC GARDENING. By the staff
   of Organic Gardening Magazine. New rev. ed.
   Emmaus, PA: Rodale Press, 1978. 1236p.
   This ambitious title is described as "an
   encyclopedia covering the whole field of
   horticulture, from the organic point of view." It
   is an alphabetically arranged encyclopedia with
   information on specific plants found under common
   name (with cross references from the botanical
   name) and with many entries of a general
   informational nature. Thus considerable
   information can be found under such subjects as

bees, strawberry, grafting, mineral rocks,
composting, sawdust, and the like. It is written
in a nontechnical manner and is practical in
intent. The most complete source on organic
gardening, it has less merit as a general
gardening encyclopedia.

77. Foster, Catharine Osgood. ORGANIC FLOWER GARDENING.
Emmaus, PA: Rodale Press, 1975. 305p.
Commonsense information on perennials, annuals,
and bulbs is given in this title oriented
toward organic growing methods. The emphasis is
on growing healthy plants in correct growing
conditions to avoid disease and pest problems.
Much practical advice in provided on designing and
constructing flower beds and also for the care and
planting of specific plants. Mrs. Foster's advice
is practical, for instance she recommends avoiding
hybrid tea roses and rather to plant roses which
are more resistant to black spot and Japanese
beetles. Practical and highly recommended.

78. THE ORGANIC GARDENER'S COMPLETE GUIDE TO VEGETABLES
AND FRUITS. From the editors of Rodale Press.
Emmaus, PA: Rodale Press, 1982. 510p.
Most organic gardeners are especially concerned
that their vegetables and fruits are grown
"naturally" with no chemical sprays or
fertilizers. This inclusive title covers both the
basics of vegetable and fruit gardening and how to
grow them organically. Raising vegetables under
intensive culture, raised beds, and containers is
discussed. Also included is information on
storing vegetable crops. The fruit gardening
section includes advice on planning, planting
techniques, propagation (including grafting),
pruning, and training. The recommended organic
pest and disease conrol measures would be of
interest only to the most dedicated organic
gardeners. Both the vegetable and fruit sections
discuss specific types of produce in depth.
Recommended varieties are listed (as of 1982).

79. THE ENCYCLOPEDIA OF NATURAL INSECT AND DISEASES
CONTROL: THE MOST COMPRHENSIVE GUIDE TO PROTECTING
PLANTS-VEGETABLES, FRUIT, FLOWERS, TREES, AND
LAWNS--WITHOUT TOXIC CHEMICALS. Edited by Roger B.
Yepsen, Jr. Emmaus, PA: Rodale Press, 1984. 490p.
Detailed information on the control of pests and
diseases for a wide variety of food plants using

organic methods is included in this large manual. Among the topics covered in this encyclopedia are resistant varieties, biological controls, traps and barriers, and companion plantings. The depth of coverage is indicated by its entry on tomatoes which discusses 12 insects and 25 diseases as being problems on tomatoes. An earlier version of this title was entitled ORGANIC PLANT PROTECTION. Since that title was published in 1976, newer "natural" control measures and agents have been added to bring this manual up-to-date.

80. Shewell-Cooper, W.E.  COMPOST GARDENING. New York: Hafner Press, 1974. 118p.
For the English perspective on organic gardening, Mr. Shewell-Cooper's title could be consulted. His specific method of making compost is detailed. He recommends spreading a thin layer of compost over the soil to produce better soil, provide nutrients, to conserve water, and to prevent the growth of weeds. Other rather chatty advice is given on such topics as companion planting, lawn making, and disease and pest control.

81. Riotte, Louise.  SECRETS OF COMPANION PLANTING. Charlotte, VT: Garden Way, 1981.
This title details companion planting in vegetable, herb, fruit, and flower gardens. It is a slight book but may be of interest to organic gardeners.

LANDSCAPE DESIGN

82. Eckbo, Garrett.  HOME LANDSCAPING: THE ART OF HOME LANDSCAPING. Rev. ed. New York: McGraw-Hill, 1978. 340p.
Mr. Eckbo defines the complexities of the landscape design process for the beginner. This revised edition which was originally published under the title, THE ART OF HOME LANDSCAPING, is well written, organized, and attractively presented. Taking the novice through the design process, Mr. Eckbo covers aesthetics, design principles and elements, plant selection, and much more. The many photographs amplify the text. Although landscape design is a detailed and

complex process and many other texts will need to
be consulted, this book is a good beginning for
most gardeners. It has a good bibliography for
those seeking other titles.

83.  Nelson, William R.  PLANTING DESIGN: A MANUAL OF
     THEORY AND PRACTICE. Champaign, IL: Stipes, 1979.
     186p.

     Design considerations are excellently introduced
     in this compact title for the beginning or
     unexperienced designer.  Design elements such as
     texture, form, line, color, repetition, variety,
     balance, emphasis, and many others are all defined
     and applied to the design process.  The
     composition process and some typical types of
     landscape plans are reviewed.  A long tabular
     listing of plant materials gives landscape
     considerations and cultural requirements.  A
     "qualities chart" also lists plant material
     arranged by design characteristics.  One of the
     most concise and usable guides for the novice
     designer.

84.  Smyser, Carol A.  NATURE'S DESIGN: A PRACTICAL GUIDE
     TO NATURAL LANDSCAPING. Emmaus, PA: Rodale Press,
     1982. 390p.

     The approach of this practical title is
     ecologically oriented, or as the author states,
     "It lets the environment shape the way humans
     interact with the landscape." The site analysis
     of the landscape is studied carefully taking into
     account its geology, physiography (the study of
     the form of the earth), hydrology (water
     concerns), soils, climate, and the existing
     vegetation and wildlife.  Next plant selection is
     covered with emphasis on natural materials and
     using these plants to modify the environment.  The
     practicalities of construction methods (grading,
     drainage, paving, etc.) are detailed.  Other
     topics covered are propagation, finding native
     plant materials, and most importantly, defining
     the lifestyles that allows for this more
     ecologically sane approach to landscape design.
     This excellent title is highly recommended to
     anyone begining the design process even if they
     will not follow all of the more natural methods
     and the aesthetics of this detailed text.

85.  Ortloff, Henry Stuart, and Henry Bond Raymore.  THE

BOOK OF LANDSCAPE DESIGN. New York: Morrow, 1975.
316p.
This title has long been recommended as a text on
beginning     design     in     reading     lists     and
bibliographies.   Chapters   divide   the   design
process   into   theory,   principles,   compositional
rules,   and then their   application.   Specifics of
site preparation and elements of the landscape are
then   introduced.   Also included are a summary of
the   history   of   landscape   architecture,   the
landscape   architect-client   relationship,   and
aspects of large scaled public designs.   Written
as   a text for the beginning design student,   this
text contains more detailed information than would
interest the average homeowner.

86.   READER'S DIGEST PRACTICAL GUIDE TO HOME LANDSCAPING.
Pleasantville, NY: The Reader's Digest Association,
1977.   479p.
This   older   title   might   be   in   many   library
collections and does     explain the design process
in   terms   most   gardeners   can   understand.
Practically   focused,   it   emphasizes   specific
projects   that   the homeowner can   incorporate   to
improve   their landscapes.   Design principles and
aesthetics   are   briefly   covered.   Its   many
photographs   and drawings might prove helpful   for
those   seeking ideas for their   landscapes.   Best
used   in   conjunction   with   other   more   detailed
texts.

87.   Wirth, Thomas.   THE VICTORY GARDEN LANDSCAPE GUIDE.
Boston: Little Brown, 1984.   360p.
Written   in the same month-by-month format as   the
other   Victory   Garden titles,   this   handsomely
illustrated   text   could   provide   many   practical
ideas   for   gardeners to incorporate   into   their
landscapes.   Principles of landscape design   are
only   very briefly covered so most gardeners   will
certainly   want   to consult other   design   titles.
Plant   selection,   building   materials,   landscape
features,   and ornaments are also discussed.   The
index will have to be consulted often.

88.   Diekelmann, John, and Robert Schuster.   NATURAL
LANDSCAPING: DESIGNING WITH NATIVE PLANT
COMMUNITIES.   New York: McGraw-Hill, 1982.   276p.
Written   to   utilize   the   native   plants   in   the
Eastern   and Midwestern portions of the U.S.,   this

attractive title gives both good advice on design
planning and descriptions of the native plant
communities found in these areas. The needs for
both humans and plants are incorporated into the
planning process. The plant communities discussed
range from dryland prairies to climax forests.
Practical, with sound advice on the design
process.

89. Ireys, Alice Recknagel. HOW TO PLAN AND PLANT YOUR
OWN PROPERTY. New York: Morrow, 1980. 182p.
Valuable for its many sample residential landscape
designs, this title should be of help to the
homeowner who wants some concrete ideas for his
landscape. The fundamentals of the design process
are covered too briefly to be of much practical
assistance, but the actual plans with their design
renderings and good photographs show many good
design ideas. This title again should be used in
conjunction with more detailed landscape design
titles.

90. Brookes, John. THE SMALL GARDEN. New York: Van
Nostrand Reinhold, 1983. 256p.
The many colorful photographs and drawings of this
popular English title excite the homeowner to the
possibilities of designing mainly urban
residential landscapes. Many different designs
are briefly described and pictured. Other texts
will have to be consulted to translate these
gardens to different landscape conditions, as the
advice on this process in this title is too brief.
Plant material cited is that which is commonly
used in England, so for most of North America
other plant materials would have to be chosen. A
good title from which to garner new ideas.

91. Nelson, William R. DESIGNING AN ENERGY-EFFICIENT HOME
LANDSCAPE. Urbana, IL: University of Illinois/
College of Agriculture/Cooperative Extension
Service, 1980. 13p.
This short extension publication alerts the
homeowner to considerations of landscape elements
that affect energy use in the home. By using
plant materials, earth, and landscape structures,
the author shows how major changes in the home's
microclimate can be made. Illustrated by
drawings.

92.  Ireys, Alice Recknagel. SMALL GARDENS FOR CITY AND
     COUNTRY: A GUIDE TO DESIGNING AND PLANTING YOUR
     GREEN SPACES. Englewood Cliffs, NJ: Prentice-Hall,
     1978. 212p.
     A short title emphasizing the possibilities of
     landscaping small properties. Divided into
     sections on city gardens and country gardens, it
     illustrates many small designs that could be
     considered. Short advice on landscape features
     (fences, lighting, terraces, walls) and a listing
     of the author's favorite plants are appended.
     Another title that would be helpful in providing
     ideas for landscapes although, again, the design
     process is too briefly covered.
93.  Hannebaum, Leroy. LANDSCAPE DESIGN: A PRACTICAL
     APPROACH. Reston, VA: Reston Pub., 1981. 392p.
     For those planning a more in depth study of the
     landscape design process or for those who want to
     become more knowledgeable in this area before
     hiring a designer or architect, this detailed
     title would be of interest. Design processes,
     land form alterations, selection of plant
     material, discussions of specifications, estimates
     and bids, and much more are covered. Not written
     for the homeowner but for the beginning design
     student.
94.  Church, Thomas Dolliver; Grace Hall; and Michael
     Laurie. GARDENS ARE FOR PEOPLE. 2d. ed.
     New York: McGraw-Hill, 1983. 256p.
     Focusing on the designs of the late American
     landscape architect, Thomas Church, this title
     helps define the design process. Site
     considerations and design elements are illustrated
     through Mr. Church's work. A series of the
     gardens he designed are featured to show how he
     worked in projects of different scale. Valuable
     both as a record of Mr. Church's famous designs
     and for the insights it gives to the design
     process. Most of the designs were designed for
     climates similar to California's. The first
     edition, while quite different, is valuable for
     the same reasons.
95.  Landphair, Harlow G., and Fred Klatt. LANDSCAPE
     ARCHITECTURE CONSTRUCTION. New York: Elsevier,
     1979. 432p.
     Technical considerations in landscape construction

are    excellently  covered in  this  manual  for
professionals.  Basic properties of various woods,
concrete,  and  masonry  are  listed  along  with
specifics on drainage,  grading,  irrigation,  and
lighting.   Schematic  drawings  detail  retaining
walls,  gates,  decks,  and  many  more  landscape
elements.   Although  this manual was written  for
landscape architects and contractors,  it contains
information  of  interest  to  the  do-it-yourself
gardener.

96.  Carpenter, Philip L.; Theodore D. Walker; and
     Frederick O. Lanphear.  PLANTS IN THE LANDSCAPE.
     San Franciso: W.H. Freeman, 1975.  481p.
     Written for the landscape industry,  this title is
     divided into     sections on the design  process,
     the implementation of landscape plans,  and  final
     maintenance  of  the  landscape.   It  gives  the
     amateur  another  perspective to  landscaping  and
     would  be  useful to the beginner in defining  the
     principles,  processes, and many practicalities of
     designing and implementing a landscape design.   It
     is a manual about this process,  but not on how to
     develop a specific landscape design.

97.  Page, Russell.  THE EDUCATION OF A GARDENER.
     New York:  Random House, 1983.  382p.
     The   combination  of  years  of   experience   in
     designing  famous     landscapes on both sides  of
     the  Atlantic  and a  carefully  controlled  prose
     style  has made this title both deservedly popular
     and highly recommended.   Not only does one  learn
     about designing landscapes and plant material, but
     it is,  of course,  entertaining to read about the
     author's  experiences in exotic  places and  famous
     gardens throughout the world.   The new edition is
     little changed from the first.

98.  Damrosch, Barbara.  THEME GARDENS.  New York:
     Workman Pub., 1982.  224p.
     Gardeners  will  have to use this  book  carefully
     because  little     information is included on  how
     to  adapt  these plans for their  own  conditions.
     Among   the   sixteen   gardens   included    are
     Shakespearen,  Victorian,  gray,  butterfly, and a
     colonial garden.   This title is useful only as it
     gives gardeners ideas for their own landscapes.

99.  Miller, Michael.  GARDENING IN SMALL SPACES.
     New York: Putnam, 1983.  160p.
     The   planning  of  small  front   gardens,   side
     passageway gardens, window boxes, balcony gardens,
     roof  gardens,  and more are briefly    covered in

this beginner's guide. Detailed plans are
featured in this English title. Taking one plan,
for example, for a front garden in the English
cottage garden style, a green skeleton for year-
around interest is proposed for both sunny and
shady locations, and then plantings for spring,
summer, fall, and winter for many different
conditions are given. The plants recommended
would have to be modified for many North American
conditions. Many colored drawings and photographs
are featured.

100. Burgess, Lorraine Marshall. GARDEN ART: THE PERSONAL
PURSUIT OF ARTISTIC REFINEMENTS, INVENTIVE CONCEPTS,
OLD FOLLIES AND NEW CONCEITS FOR THE HOME GARDENER.
New York: Walker, 1981. 192p.
The use of structures and ornaments in the
landscape is introduced in this attractively
illustrated title. Art, fences, gazebos, benches,
weather vanes, specimen plants, and much more are
pictured. Construction methods are ignored.

101. Foley, Daniel J. THE COMPLETE BOOK OF GARDEN
ORNAMENTS, COMPLEMENTS AND ACCESSORIES. New York:
Crown, 1972. 247p.
An older title that pictures many different
examples of garden art, ornaments, and
structures. Garden furniture, pots, fences,
gates, sculpture, pools, and much more are
pictured. Construction methods are again ignored.

102. Oldale, Adrienne, and Peter Oldale. GARDEN
CONSTRUCTION IN PICTURES. New York: Drake Pub.,
1974. 160p.
Good photographs lead the gardener into do-it-
yourself construction projects such as fences,
compost bins, cold frames, and patios. Details
are illustrated well. A novice would have to
consult other more detailed titles to read further
on the properties of wood, concrete, etc. There
are many similar books that cover the same subject
matter.

## Specialty Gardens

### Rock Gardening and Alpines
(see also publications (553) of the American Rock
Garden Society)

103. Foster, H. Lincoln. ROCK GARDENING: A GUIDE TO

GROWING ALPINES AND OTHER WILDFLOWERS IN THE
AMERICAN GARDEN. Portland, OR: Timber Press, 1982.
Written by one of the deans of American rock
gardeners, this practical handbook is an excellent
introduction to rock gardening for American
gardeners. Its practicality is evidenced by the
glossary that precedes the text. Rock garden
construction, the construction of alpine houses,
and general cultural information on these
speciality gardens are given detailed treatment.
The alphabetical listing of genera includes much
practical observation and experience with these
plants in eastern American growing conditions.
The best guide for American gardeners.

104.  Foster, Raymond. ROCK GARDEN & ALPINE PLANTS.
North Pomfret, VT: David & Charles, 1982. 256p.
An interesting approach to rock gardens and their
plants, as the text is arranged by chapters
describing many different native alpine plant
habitats. Thus plants are grouped together by
similar cultural requirements whether it is plants
from the Mediterranean, Canada and the North,
those growing east of Missouri, or from many other
regions. There are brief discussions of rock
garden construction and culture. Appended is a
very useful table that lists form, flower, height,
soil, and site requirements of the plants
discussed. The text has charm and makes good
reading. An excellent English title.

105.  Heath, Royton E. THE COLLINGRIDGE GUIDE TO
COLLECTORS' ALPINES: THEIR CULTIVATION IN FRAMES
AND ALPINE HOUSES. Beaverton, OR: Timber
Press, 1983. 543p.
This detailed text for the alpine specialist
combines both general discusssions on types of
alpine gardens and detailed listings of the plants
grown as alpines. Alpine houses and frames are
described with also good discussions of pans,
soils, propagation methods, and general
maintenance information. The plants described
are divided into dwarf conifers, and a general
listing of other alpines giving good descriptions,
blooming time, native habitat, and keyed
information indicating what type of cultivation
methods are required. One of the best reference

works on these plants and also a good handbook on
alpine houses. Alpine houses are rare in most
sections of North America, but this English title
is one of the most useful texts on the subject.

106. Harkness, Bernard E. THE SEEDLIST HANDBOOK. 3rd. ed.
Bellona, NY: Kashong, 1980. 246p.
This compact guide leads one to information on
thousands of rock    garden plants. Compiled from
the seed lists offered to members of the American
Rock Garden Society, the Alpine Garden Society
(England), and the Scottish Rock Garden Club, it
briefly describes each generic listing and states
where more detailed descriptions can be found in a
large number of reference works and speciality
rock gardening titles. An extremely useful
reference tool.

107. Heath, Royton E. ROCK PLANTS FOR SMALL GARDENS. New
York: Collingridge, 1982. [Dist. by Hamlyn]. 144p.
Alpine trough construction and the general
selection and care of    smaller sized rock garden
plants are included in this popular English title.
After a short chapter on conifers, rock, and
alpine plants are listed in a tabular descriptive
list. This list includes the plant's suitability
for different growing conditions, containers,
propagation, height and spread, what soils are
recommended, and more. This listing is
alphabetical by genus. This title was first
published under the title, MINIATURE ROCK
GARDENING.

108. Ingwersen, Will. INGWERSEN'S MANUAL OF ALPINE PLANTS.
Eastbourne, England: author/Dunnsprint, 1978. 445p.
Written by one of England's most renowned
plantsmen, this    encyclopedic alphabetical title
lists genera suitable for rock gardens and alpine
house culture. For each genus, a brief
description is given along with cultural advice.
Primary species are selected and described. A
personal selection of those plants that the author
has found of merit.

109. Bloom, Alan. ALPINES FOR YOUR GARDEN. Chicago:
Floraprint U.S.A., 1981. 128p.
A pictorial listing of rock garden plants compiled
by a noted    English garden writer. Color
photographs are featured with brief descriptions
and how the plants are best used and grown. A

general discussion of rock gardening and alpine
house culture is given in the introduction. Also
lists of plants for specific purposes are
appended. Useful mainly as a pictorial
encyclopedia of over 200 of these plants.
110. Tanner, Ogden. ROCK AND WATER GARDENS. The Time-Life
Encyclopedia of Gardening. Alexandria, VA:
Time-Life Books, 1982. 160p.
As in other works in this series, this short book
combines information on rock and water gardens
and would be a good introduction to these
specialty gardens. Construction is briefly
covered along with many good photographs which
could excite one to the possibilities of these
gardens in the landscape. The encyclopedic
listing of suitable plants gives brief descriptive
and cultural information along with the usual
small color drawings of each plant.
111. Stites, Jerry S., and Robert G. Mower. ROCK GARDENS.
Ithaca, NY: New York State College of Agriculture
and Life Sciences, 1979? Information Bulletin
no. 159. 29p.
For an introduction to rock gardens and a few of
the more popular rock garden plants this extension
publication is an economical purchase. Fifty of
the more common rock garden plants are illustrated
with color photographs. They are also briefly
described with flowering and foliage
characteristics, cultivation requirements, and
propagation methods. Brief introductory materials
discuss general rock garden construction.

Gardening in the Shade

112. Schenk, George. THE COMPLETE SHADE GARDENER. Boston:
Houghton Mifflin, 1984. 278p.
This positive title introduces many trees, shrubs,
vines, ferns, perennials, annuals and "edibles"
that will grow well in the shade. The author
personally evaluates these plants, for instance he
rates the silver maple, "maybe the worst of all
garden trees in the United States." The landscape
plants are evaluated for their use throughout most
of the U.S. including subtropical climates. There
are about 200 pages of plant evaluations. Also
included are excellent chapters on the

construction of shade gardens, pruning, and pests
and diseases. Highly recommended.

113. Pierot, Suzanne Warner. WHAT CAN I GROW IN THE SHADE?
New York: Liveright, 1977. 221p.

The title aptly describes this book, as the author
describes the many annuals, perennials, ferns,
ground covers, shrubs, bulbs, and vines that do
best in more shaded locations. This American
author emphasizes that shady conditions also mean
conditions with not enough humus, water, or air
circulation. Advice on correcting these
deficiencies and also for constructing woodland
gardens are included. In the appendix shade-
loving plants are grouped by U.S. climatic region.
A practical, positive title.

114. Allen, Oliver E. SHADE GARDENS. The Time-Life
Encyclopedia of Gardening. Alexandria, VA:
Time-Life, 1979. 160p.

The encyclopedic section of this title lists more
common shrubs, perennials, ferns, bulbs, annuals,
ground covers, and small trees that do best in
shade. Brief descriptions and cultural advice are
listed for each plant. The introductory pictorial
essays excite the gardener to the possibilities of
growing plants in the shade. Good ideas and brief
advice are highlighted.

115. Paterson, Allen. PLANTS FOR SHADE. London:
J.M. Dent, 1981. 214p.

For an English gardening perspective, this title
might be of interest to serious gardeners. Plants
grown in Britain are 115 accurately described and
advice is given on how they can best be used in
the shaded garden. An added feature is the
description of plants that provide interest month-
by-month throughout the year.

## Water Gardening

116. Perry, Frances. THE WATER GARDEN. New York:
Van Nostrand Reinhold, 1981. 176p.

Frances Perry's first book on water gardening was
published in England in 1938 and has gone through
many editions since then. Expert advice on garden
construction and water plants is given. Water
lilies, different types of aquatic plants

and bog garden plants are described in depth.
American gardeners will have to translate
information on these plants and gardens for their
less temperate conditions.

117. Ledbetter, Gordon T. WATER GARDENS. New York:
W.W. Norton, 1980. 152p.
Another English title that is especially useful
for the design of water gardens. Well
illustrated, it shows many good ideas for the
construction of these gardens. The chapters on
water plants are accessed best by using the index.
Other features include fish and "livestock" for
the water garden and a day-by-day diary taking
such a garden through the year.

* Tanner, Ogden. ROCK AND WATER GARDENS. Cited above
as item 110.

118. Muhlberg, Helmut. THE COMPLETE GUIDE TO WATER PLANTS:
A REFERENCE BOOK. New York: EP Pub., 1982.
[Dist. by Sterling Pub.] 391p.
After introducing the general cultivation of
aquatic plants, how they grow, and their
propagation techniques, Muhlberg provides a
detailed listing of many of the world's cultivated
aquatic plants. The encyclopedic section of
plants is arranged by family with the important
genera and species listed. Distribution, plant
characteristics, and general information on their
use in aquatic gardens and aquaria are included.
Numerous color and black and white photographs are
featured. This title is best used as a reference
to many aquatic plants and used in conjunction
with other titles on water gardening. It has
little advice on planting and care.

119. Swindells, Philip. WATERLILIES. Portland, OR:
Timber Press, 1983. 159p.
Although culture of waterlilies is oriented toward
English conditions, this up-to-date monograph will
be of interest to those with water gardens.
Hardy day and night tropical waterlilies are
described. Unfortunately, their relative
hardiness is not defined. The gigantic Victoria,
nuphars, and nelumbos are also described. Pool
construction and waterlily culture are well
covered.

* Huxley, Anthony, ed. GARDEN PERENNIALS AND WATER
PLANTS. Cited below as (156).

Wildflower Gardening & Gardening with Native Plants

120.   Steffek, Edwin Frances.  THE NEW WILD FLOWERS AND HOW
       TO GROW THEM.  Enl. and rev. ed.  Portland, OR:
       Timber Press, 1983.  186p.
       A useful guide to the cultivation of wildflowers.
       The detailed   encyclopedic section is   arranged
       by  common name (for  instance,  the  asters,  the
       bluebells).   Description,   native   habitat,
       indication of  primary and secondary species  for
       garden  interest,  and  cultural  information  is
       included.  Small, variable quality black-and-white
       photographs  and  some  color  photographs   are
       featured.   Practical in emphasis and designed for
       the  amateur.  Expensive  for a  paperback!   The
       first edition still has value.
121.   Taylor, Kathryn S. and Stephen F. Hambin.  HANDBOOK OF
       WILD FLOWER CULTIVATION.  New York: Collier Books,
       1976.  307p.
       Although  first published in  1963,  this  popular
       handbook  still has   much to offer those seeking
       information on wildflower gardening.  The authors
       describe   wild  flower  species  by  family   and
       evaluate   their   use   in   the   wild   garden.
       Propagation methods are indicated for each.  Small
       line   drawings  help  in  their   identification.
       Introductory   chapters  concentrate  on   general
       methods  of propagation.  To find out  what  wild
       flowers  to  grow  for  specific  locations,   the
       authors  append many lists of wild flowers defined
       by their cultural requirements.
122.   Miles, Bebe.  WILDFLOWER PERENNIALS FOR YOUR GARDEN:
       A DETAILED GUIDE TO YEARS OF BLOOM FROM AMERICA'S
       LONG-NEGLECTED NATIVE HERITAGE.  New York:
       Hawthorn Books, 1976.  294p.
       Restricted  to  100  native  American  perennials
       (biased   toward   eastern   North   American
       wildflowers),  this title would be very useful for
       those  selecting  plants for  wildflower  gardens.
       The discussion of the 100 wildflowers are  divided
       into  three sections,  plants for sunny locations,
       for shady sites,  and wet spots.   For each plant,
       family,  genus,  and species are listed along with
       habitat,  description,  blooming period,  culture,
       and  related  species.   Advice is provided on  the
       planning and preparation of  wildflower  gardens.

The excellent wildflower line drawings are by H.
Peter Loewer.

123. Bruce, Hal. HOW TO GROW WILDFLOWERS AND WILD SHRUBS
AND TREES IN YOUR OWN GARDEN. New York:
Van Nostrand Reinhold, 1982. 299p.
Personal observation on many of the eastern North
American wild plants highlights this book.
Informally written and arranged, it is best read
straight through to mine its considerable
information. Indication of its focus is given in
the chapter titles which include "winter trees,"
"yellow daisies," "high summer," and "shrubs in
the woodland." As the title indicates, useful
information on native trees and shrubs is also
included. The good index should be consulted
often.

124. Crockett, James Underwood and Oliver E. Allen.
WILDFLOWER GARDENING. The Time-Life Encyclopedia
of Gardening. Alexandria, VA: Time-Life, 1977. 160p.
Divided into two sections, an encyclopedic listing
of plants and introductory chapters, this title
provides a short introduction to wild flower
gardening. The encyclopedic section presents
tasteful color illustrations of each genus
included with also nontechnical descriptions of
the plants, indications of where they are native,
and brief information on how to grow them.
Introductory chapters explore the possibilities of
wild flower gardening.

125. Schmidt, Marjorie G. GROWING CALIFORNIA NATIVE
PLANTS. Berkeley: University of California Press,
1980. California Natural History Guides, #45. 366p.
This title is an example of the many regional
guides that advocate the cultivation of native
wild plants. Here chapters on native annuals,
perennials, bulbs, shrubs and trees are followed
by lists of the uses of these plants. Information
on genera include habit, foliage, flowers, fruit,
distribution, garden uses and culture. Species
with more landscape merit are discussed in depth
while other species are given shorter treatment.
Many genera are described in detailed charts.
Chapters on propagation and general culture are
included. Appended are source lists and
references. This is a model monograph on the uses
of wild plants for specific climatic areas.

126. DIRECTORY TO RESOURCES ON WILDLFOWER PROPAGATION.
Prepared by Gene A. Sullivan and Richard H. Daley.
St. Louis: National Council of State Garden Clubs,
1981. 331p.
This detailed study will be of interest to wild
flower specialists. Produced under the auspices
of the National Council of State Garden Clubs, it
divides the United States into six growing regions
and indicates which propagation techniques are
used for specific wildflowers. For each region
the plants are arranged by family with indication
of such information as seed treatment, soil
moisture, flowering times, and height. Information
is given in chart form. A good index is included
in this landmark title.

127. Kruckeberg, Arthur R. GARDENING WITH NATIVE PLANTS OF
THE PACIFIC NORTHWEST: AN ILLUSTRATED GUIDE.
Seattle: U. of Washington Press, 1982. 252p.
For the Pacific Northwest, native trees, shrubs,
perennials and ferns are described, pictured, and
given landscape use. The illustrations include
both photographs and line drawings to aid in
identification. The author's descriptions and
cultural advice are detailed and specific from
close personal observation and experience in
cultivating these plants. Appended are lists of
plants for specific purposes, sources, a glossary
and bibliography.

128. Duffield, Mary Rose, and Warren D. Jones. PLANTS FOR
DRY CLIMATES: HOW TO SELECT, GROW AND ENJOY.
Tucson, AZ: H.P. Books, 1981. 176p.
After defining the challenges of growing plants in
arid climates, this paperback lists those plants
that would be suitable for these climatic
conditions. Generally this region as defined by
this title stretches from southern California
through western Texas. Plants are arranged
alphabetically by genus with landscape use,
relative merits, cultural information, and modern
cultivars listed. Many small color photographs
are included. Coverage of plant material ranges
from grass to trees.

129. Penn, Cordelia. LANDSCAPING WITH NATIVE PLANTS.
Winston-Salem, NC: John F. Blair, 1982. 226p.
For those gardening in the Piedmont region of the
Appalachians, this specific title details the

native trees, shrubs, vines, and wildflowers that
can be utilized in the landscape. Advice is
included on landscape design and the care and
maintenance of these plants. An illustrated
glossary is appended.

## Container Gardening
(see also vegetable gardening)

130. Yang, Linda. THE TERRACE GARDENER'S HANDBOOK: RAISING
PLANTS ON A BALCONY, TERRACE, ROOFTOP, PENTHOUSE OR
PATIO. Beaverton, OR: Timber Press, 1982. 283p.
Gardeners do not always have unlimited space or
good growing conditions so this text, subtitled
"raising plants on a balcony, terrace, rooftop,
penthouse or patio" can be very useful. Filled
with information on soil mixes, types of
containers, and recommended plants for this type
of gardening, it is a practical text. Maintenance
procedures for all times of the year and for
periodic renewal of the plantings are covered in
depth. Possible problems with hardiness of plants
in containers are discussed.

## Color in Gardens
(Although there are older classic titles by
Gertrude Jekyll and Louise Beebe Wilder, the
titles below will be of more practical use for the
gardener.)

131. Haring, Elda. COLOR FOR YOUR YARD & GARDEN.
New York: Hawthorn: Books, 1971. 240p.
Color from flowers, fruits, or foliage of
landscape material is included in this
practical title. In the main section the
discussions of plant material is broken down by
landscape color. For each plant, genus, common
name, growing height, why the plant is useful for
color, and a color photograph of the plant are
included. Short chapters on seasonal
considerations are also given. Lists of plants by
color, by fragrance, by effective combinations of
such plants, and a quick reference chart for
selection purposes are also appended.
132. Underwood, Desmond, Mrs. GREY AND SILVER PLANTS.
London: Collins, 1971. 143p.

Although this title is out of print and hard to
obtain, it is an excellent guide to grey and
silver hued plants. The discussion of these
plants is arranged alphabetically by genus.
Listed are origin, habit, hardiness (for England),
use, planting time, propagation, and much personal
information. This title is charming, well written
and designed.

133. Simmons, Adelma Grenier. THE SILVER GARDEN.
     Coventry, CT: Caprilands Herb Farm, n.d. 103p.
     After briefly describing three different small
     gardens built upon grey hued plants, this well
     known author on herbs lists the many plants that a
     gardener could use. Much first-hand knowledge on
     the culture and use of these plants is given.
     Appended in this small paperback are some culinary
     recipes for a midsummer's eve party in a silver
     garden.

## Fragrance in Gardens

134. Verey, Rosemary. THE SCENTED GARDEN. New York:
     Van Nostrand Reinhold, 1981. 168p.
     This knowledgeable English writer's descriptions
     of fragrant plants includes much personal
     observation. Although the book contains plants
     not commonly grown or available in many parts of
     North America, it is a very useful text. Divided
     broadly into types of fragrant plants (bulbs,
     roses, herbs), it discusses both which plants to
     grow and how to use them. Appended are lists of
     plants with scented leaves, flowers, a fragrant
     seasonal breakdown, scented evening plants,
     scented plants for culinary uses and more.
     Although a practical volume, this title is also
     enjoyable to read or browse through.

135. Wilson, Helen Van Pelt. THE FRAGRANT YEAR: SCENTED
     PLANTS FOR YOUR GARDEN AND YOUR HOME. New York:
     M. Barrows, 1967. 306p.
     This older title is useful for its American bias.
     Plants are divided by broad chapters such as
     fragrant winter plants, early bulbs and small
     perennials, "autumn aromas," and more. Wilson
     always writes from personal experience so there is
     much practical advice included.

136.    Sanecki, Kay N. THE FRAGRANT GARDEN. London:
        Batsford, 1981. 166p.
            Using a historical approach, this is another
            English title on fragrant plants. Excellent
            introductory chapters on the history of scent
            in gardens leads one into the construction of
            these gardens. The author's encyclopedic listing
            of fragrant plants is broken down into greenhouse
            plants, bulbs, shrubs, green aromatics, trees, and
            others. Again this text's English bias may prove
            to be a problem to North American gardeners.
137.    Genders, Roy. SCENTED FLORA OF THE WORLD. New York:
        St. Martin's Press, 1977. 534p.
            For those looking for more detailed information on
            scented plants of the world, this title might be
            of interest. After a short history of the uses of
            fragrant plants, a detailed classified listing of
            many of the scented plants of the world is
            featured. Chapters list plants with scented
            fruits, roots, leaves, and much more along with
            lists of plants by types of plants (shrubs, trees,
            annuals, etc). A very comprehensive guide.

                              Seasonal Bloom
            (Many titles on color in the garden also cover
            this subject. Generally the titles below
            emphasize color in winter when many
            landscapes lack interest.)


138.    Wilson, Helen Van Pelt. COLOR FOR YOUR WINTER YARD &
        GARDEN, WITH FLOWERS, BERRIES, BIRDS, AND TREES.
        New York: Scribner, 1978. 175p.
            This attractive title emphasizes seasonal plants
            and such landscape enhancements as garden
            lighting to add interest to the winter garden.
            Bulbs, trees, shrubs, and perennials are included.
            Another subject covered in this attractive title
            is attracting birds to the landscape with food-
            producing plants. Another excellent title by Mrs.
            Wilson.
139.    Allen, Oliver E. WINTER GARDENS. The Time-Life
        Encyclopedia of Gardening. Alexandria, VA:
        Time-Life Books, 1979. 160p.
            One of the better books in this series because the
            more limited subject is treated in greater

depth. Included are a generic encyclopedic
listing of those plants that add interest to the
winter landscape. Small drawings, brief
description, and cultural information are given
for each generic listing. Introductory chapters
define features for the winter landscape and "in
pursuit of year-round bloom." Fall and winter
garden tasks are also discussed.

140. Thomas, Graham Stuart. COLOUR IN THE WINTER GARDEN.
3rd. ed. London: J.M. Dent, 1984.
Mr. Thomas's title lists shrubs, trees, heathers,
rhododendrons, and bulbs that are used in England
to provide seasonal interest in winter. North
American gardeners will find unfamiliar plant
material included. For experienced gardeners.

141. Foster, Raymond. THE GARDEN IN AUTUMN AND WINTER.
North Pomfret, VT: David & Charles, 1983. 232p.
Attractively illustrated, this English title
should be of interest to experienced gardeners.
After a discussion of basic planning, the author
described bulbs, perennials, shrubs, trees, and
vines for the winter landscape. Chapters on
autumn and winter flowers, attractive winter
stems, plants with attractive fruit, and more are
included.


ORNAMENTAL GARDENING PLANTS

Perennials and Annuals

142. Wilson, Helen Van Pelt. SUCCESSFUL GARDENING WITH
PERENNIALS: HOW TO SELECT AND GROW MORE THAN 500
KINDS FOR TODAY'S YARD AND GARDEN.
Garden City, NY: Doubleday, 1976. 289p.
Helen Van Pelt Wilson is one of America's best
garden writers. Her books now are unfortunately
somewhat out of date and also are out of print.
This is one of the last titles that she wrote and
is still one of the best perennial manuals. It is
not only a guide to specific perennials and their
culture but also provides useful instruction on
how to create and maintain a perennial garden.
The basics of perennial gardening are detailed in
such chapters as "the indispensable daylily,"
"good edging for good looks," "where shade

prevails" and "foliage peacemakers". A choice
title on perennial garden design and the selection
of perennial plant material.

143. Free, Montague. ALL ABOUT THE PERENNIAL GARDEN; THE
AMATEUR GARDENER'S HANDBOOK OF HARDY FLOWERS:
HERBACEOUS AND WOODY PERENNIALS, INCLUDING BULBS
AND SHRUBS, BIENNIALS AND ANNUALS. Garden City, NY:
Doubleday, 1955. 352p.
Excellent    discussions    on    designing    and
constructing  perennial  gardens  highlight  this
older title.   One particulary instructive chapter
follows  the  progress  of a  trial perennial  garden
through  an  entire  year.  Although  Mr.  Free's
listing  of recommended perennials is out of  date
(especially for cultivars),  the author's lists of
perennials for specific purposes are still useful.
Its  American   bias  also makes this   title   still
valuable.

144. Thomas, Graham Stuart. PERENNIAL GARDEN PLANTS: OR,
THE MODERN FLORILEGIUM: A CONCISE ACCOUNT OF
HERBACEOUS PLANTS, INCLUDING BULBS, FOR GENERAL
GARDEN USE. 2nd. ed. Totowa, NJ: J.M. Dent,
1983. 288p.
One of  the best gardening  books,  this  English
title contains much first hand knowledge about  an
exhaustive  listing  of  herbaceous  plants.    It
covers   over   2,000   species   of   perennials,
ornamental grasses and ferns cultivated in England
although  it omits  cultivars of such large  genera
as Chrysanthemum,  Dahlia and Gladiolus.  For most
plants  indications of family,  major species  and
cultivars  with  flower  color,  flowering  period,
growing  height,  propagation methods,  and  clear
descriptions  are  included.   The  hybridizer  or
native   habitat  is  also  usually  given.    The
encyclopedic  sections are truly  impressive  with
careful  descriptions  of the many  species  along
with  helpful advice  for use  in  the  garden.   The
new   edition   contains   corrections  with   some
additions.   The color plates have been reproduced
with much clearer color than those in the original
American  edition.   This  is  the  most  complete
modern listing of perennials.

145. Hudak, Joseph. GARDENING WITH PERENNIALS MONTH BY
MONTH. New York: Quadrangle/ New York Times Books,
1976. 398p.

This month-by-month description of blooming
perennials is very useful for the selection and
design of gardens. Cultural information for each
perennial is brief. There are good discussions of
specific cultivars of included perennials (as of
1976). Appended are lists of perennials for
specific purposes such as for shade, for longer
bloom, etc. Very useful when used with other
perennial titles.

146. Buckley, A.R. CANADIAN GARDEN PERENNIALS. Saanichton,
BC: Hancock House, 1977. 212p.
With emphasis on the hardiest perennials, this
Canadian guide is a good selection tool for the
more northern perennial gardens. The author was
horticulturist with the Canada Department of
Agriculture for 35 years. Although perennial
selection is stressed, some cultural information
is given. Color photographs help identify many
perennials. Four sample perennial border plans
should help the gardener plan perennial gardens.
Many cultivars are listed.

147. Bloom, Alan. PERENNIALS FOR YOUR GARDEN. Ed. by
Derek Fell. Chicago: Floraprint U.S.A., 1981. 133p.
Mr. Bloom's practical growing experience with the
perennials he describes makes this text especially
valuable. Advice such as "rather untidy plants
which need curbing" and "young plants are easier
to establish than old" is not often found in
perennial guides. While the color photographs are
great, Mr. Bloom's chatty advice is the star here.
An English title emphasizing commonly grown
English perennials. Inadequate index.

148. Crockett, James Underwood. CROCKETT'S FLOWER GARDEN.
Boston: Little, Brown, 1981. 311p.
As in the author's popular CROCKETT'S VICTORY
GARDEN, gardening is covered by a month-by-month
arrangement. This arrangement necessitates
constant use of the index for specific
information. The gardening information given is
from Mr. Crockett's many years of practical
growing experience so it is attractive to most
home gardeners. Colorful photography illustrate
the many garden flowers discussed. Annuals,
perennials, biennials, and bulbs are included.
This title was edited and completed after Mr.

Crockett's death.

149.    Hebb, Robert S.  LOW MAINTENANCE PERENNIALS.  New York:
        Quadrangle/ New York Times Books, 1973.  220p.
        An upbeat title emphasizing the ease of perennial
        gardening.  It is most useful for its discussion
        of specific perennials, less so for the
        construction, design, and maintenance of these
        gardens.  For each perennial included, good
        description, cultural requirements, and uses in
        the garden are given.  A selection of cultivars
        and sources for specific plants are given (as of
        1975).  Perhaps this small paperback too
        optimistically describes the ease of growing
        perennials, but it does contain good information
        on the growing and selection of perennials.
150.    Crockett, James Underwood.  ANNUALS.
        The Time-Life Encyclopedia of Gardening.
        Alexandria, Va:  Time-Life, 1971.  176p.
        Free-flowering annuals are included with brief
        cultural information and colored illustrations
        in this title.  A glossy photographic section
        shows how to use annuals in the landscape.  Sound
        suggestions on seed sowing are given.  A
        beginner's guide.
151.    Crockett, James Underwood.  PERENNIALS.  The Time-Life
        Encyclopedia of Gardening.  Alexandria, VA:
        Time-Life, 1972.  160p.
        Colored illustrations of the more commonly grown
        perennials in North America are combined with
        brief descriptions of these plants and adequate
        cultural advice.  The design and construction of
        perennial gardens are also briefly covered.  A
        guide for beginners.
152.    Faust, Joan Lee.  THE NEW YORK TIMES BOOK OF ANNUALS
        AND PERENNIALS.  New York: Times Books, 1980.  274p.
        For gardeners seeking very brief information on
        flower gardens and their plants, Joan Lee Faust's
        title would be helpful.  It contains two
        encyclopedic listings of annuals and perennials.
        Brief descriptive information, cultural advice,
        and very stylized colored drawings of the plants
        are included.  A more detailed treatment is given
        to the actual planning and construction of flower
        gardens in many different conditions.
153.    Nehrling, Arno, and Irene Nerhling.  THE PICTURE BOOK
        OF ANNUALS.  New York: Arco Pub., 1977.  288p.

This is one of the most complete guides to
annuals. It features practical advice on sowing
annuals from seed and general care of annuals. A
long section details all the annuals of ornamental
merit (here cultivar information is, of course,
out of date). The use of annuals as features of
the flower garden, as vines, for cutting, for
containers, and even as house plants is included.
Pest and disease control measures are also out-of-
date.

154. Snyder, Leon C. FLOWERS FOR NORTHERN GARDENS.
Minneapolis: University of Minnesota Press, 1983.
385p.

Northern gardeners will find this text very useful
as it delineates those perennials, annuals, and
bulbs that can be successfully grow in the North.
Arranged alphabetically by genus, each entry
describes the major species, cultivars, and
hybrids that gardeners should consider for their
conditions. It also includes specific cultural
advice and use of these plants in the landscape.
Numerous lists of flowering plants for specific
purposes are included. There are many small color
photographs.

155. Huxley, Anthony, ed. GARDEN ANNUALS AND BULBS.
New York: Macmillan, 1971. Garden Flowers in
Color, vol 1. 208p.

540 plants were originally described by the Danish
garden writer, Eigel Kiaer, with illustrations
drawn by Verner Hancke. This edition is edited by
the English garden authority, Anthony Huxley.
Annuals and bulbs are illustrated separately and
arranged alphabetically by botanical name. This
work is mainly a pictorial directory with clear
and colorful drawings. Descriptions include
growth habit, growing height, and general culture.
A series of silhouette drawings that show growth
habit of these plants in garden situations is a
unique feature. Also unusual are the drawings of
bulbs, tubers, and root shapes of the described
bulbous plants.

156. Huxley, Anthony, ed. GARDEN PERENNIALS AND WATER
PLANTS. New York: Macmillan, 1971. Garden Flowers
in Color, vol 2. 216p.

Similiar to other titles in this series, this
small, handy book would be useful to novice

gardeners for the identification of perennials and
water plants. Colorful, attractive drawings help
identify 426 species and varieties of these
plants. The text is very brief. Also included
are silhouettes of the plants as they would appear
in the garden.

157. Nicholson, Beverly Evelyn, illus. THE OXFORD BOOK OF
GARDEN FLOWERS. London: Oxford University Press,
1963. 207p.
Herbaceous plants grown commonly in English
gardens are shown in colored drawings.
Arranged by season of bloom, annuals, bulbs,
perennials, vines, and showy shrubs are
illustrated, described, and recommended for
specific purposes. American gardeners have to
translate this cultural information for their own
growing conditions. Valuable for its seasonal
blooming breakdown and for its colorful
illustrations by B.E. Nicholson.

158. BULBS AND PERENNIALS. Edited by Julie Grace.
Portland, OR: Timber Press, 1984.
Six hundred and fifteen color photographs of
mostly uncommon, less hardy perennials and bulbs
make this a valuable identification manual.
Produced in New Zealand for the identification of
ornamentals more commonly grown in the southern
hemisphere, this guide should be used in
conjunction with a garden encyclopedia to give
hardiness in other areas. (Some of these plants
will be recognized by American gardeners as indoor
plants.) Although commonly grown perennials and
bulbs (chrysanthemum, dahlia, iris, gladiolus) are
included, its discussion of more unusual plants
(TRITELEIA, VELTHEMIA, BRODIAEA, DIERAMA) makes
this guide useful. The lists of plants for sunny,
dry, and shady conditions might be useful in
similar climatic conditions such as for parts of
California. The 1967 edition written by Richmond
E. and Charles R. Harrison was the last edition
seen by the reviewer.

159. Schuler, Stanley. THE GARDENER'S BASIC BOOK OF FLOWERS.
New York: Simon & Schuster, 1974. 285p.
Annuals, perennials, biennials, and bulbs are all
covered in this general gardening manual. There
are not very many one volume works that cover
these specific plant materials, so this

title is of interest to beginners. Because of the
many plants this title covers, each entry is very
brief. This general book might contain enough
information for beginning gardeners starting a
flower garden.

160. Ingwersen, Will. CLASSIC GARDEN PLANTS. Portland, OR:
Timber Press, 1980. 192p.
Mr. Ingwersen, one of England's most renowned
contemporary plantsmen, selects those plants he
has found to be of "well-proven garden
worthiness." Personal observation of growth
habit, desired characteristics, and some cultural
requirements (for England) are included. Some of
the many illustrations are in color. The work is
of interest to more knowledgeable gardeners.
Alphabetically arranged by botanical name with no
index.

161. Giles, F.A.; Rebecca McIntosh Keith; and Donald C.
Saupe. HERBACEOUS PERENNIALS. Reston, VA:
Reston Pub., 1980. 356p.
Perennials and bulbs are listed with their related
species and varieties giving basic cultural
information and garden value. The line drawings
are simplified. Cultural information is adequate
but little information is given for diseases or
pests. Simply a listing, with no basics of
perennial garden planning, design, or maintenance.

162. Beckett, Kennth A. GROWING HARDY PERENNIALS. London:
Croom Helm, 1981. 182p.
Perennials hardy in England are briefly described
in this compact title. An encyclopedic section
lists perennial genera with selected species and
cultivars. Short discussions of culture,
propagation, and the designing of perennial
gardens preface the listing of perennials.
Appended are lists of perennials for specific
purposes and a common name index. PERENNIAL
GARDEN PLANTS by Graham Thomas (144) covers the
subject with more style and in much greater depth.

Specific Perennials

CARNATIONS
(gardening encyclopedias such as Everett (38)
contain more valuable information than the
following title)

163.  Bishop, Steven.  CARNATIONS.  New York: Sterling
      Pub., 1982.  215p.
      Concentrating  on  greenhouse  carnations,  this
      English  title  details  cultural  requirements,
      propagation,  and  growing  carnations  for
      exhibition.  Outdoor  carnation  and  pink
      cultivation  under  English  conditions  is  also
      covered.  For greenhouse growers of carnations.

CHRYSANTHEMUMS
(see also the publications (605-12) and quarterly
(542) from the National Chrysanthemum Society)

164.  Ackerson, Cornelius.  THE COMPLETE BOOK OF
      CHRYSANTHEMUMS.  Garden City, NY: Doubleday, 1957.  256p.
      Chrysanthemum  growing  in North American  gardens
      differs greatly    from the culture of this  plant
      in Europe.   Therefore,  this older American title
      will  give  American  gardeners  more  of  the
      information  they  are seeking than newer  English
      titles.  Both  general cultivation  outdoors  and
      greenhouse culture are treated in depth.  Some of
      the  information included is outdated (such as the
      recommendations of DDT),  but this is  still  the
      best  title  specifically  on  chrysanthemums  for
      American gardeners.
165.  Smith, James Francis.  CHRYSANTHEMUMS.  New York:
      Hippocrene Books, 1975.  207p.
      The  English  method  of growing  and  classifying
      chrysanthemums  (both different than the  American
      method  and  classification) is discussed in  this
      up-to-date title.   Lifting chrysanthemums in  the
      fall  and  wintering them over in  greenhouses  or
      frames is discussed.   For dedicated chrysanthemum
      growers  or for those enjoying climatic conditions
      similar to England.
166.  Randall, Harry, and Alan Wren.  GROWING CHRYSANTHEMUMS.
      Beaverton, OR: Timber Press, 1983.  168p.
      Another  English  title  for  the  chrysanthemum
      specialist.   Exhibition-type  chrysanthemums  are
      followed  from  starting  the  cuttings  from
      greenhouse  overwintered  parent  plants  through
      flowering.   Disbudding,  potting,  timing,  and
      special insights into producing exhibition quality
      specimens are covered in depth.

167. Machin, Barrie John, and Nigel Eric Anthony Scopes.
     CHRYSANTHEMUMS: THE YEAR-ROUND. Poole:
     Blandford Press, 1978. 233p.
     This more technical text focuses on growing
     chrysanthemums in the greenhouse. Commerical
     scale cut flower and pot plant production is
     detailed. Amateurs growing chrysanthemums in
     greenhouses will find some of their technical
     questions answered.

## DAHLIAS
(see also the quarterly (544) of the American
Dahlia Society, for older pre-1969 cultivars see
the listing under the Royal Horticultural Society.)

168. Hammett, Keith. THE WORLD OF DAHLIAS. Rutland, VT:
     Tuttle, 1980. 132p.
     Mr. Hammett's text covers growing dahlias in many
     locations and in many different climatic
     conditions, not just his native England or his
     adopted country, New Zealand. Therefore he gives
     good general cultural advice on soil types, types
     of propagation, and recommended storage areas. He
     succinctly classifies the many dahlia flower types
     and gives good advice on growing them for show.
     Also included is a discussion of breeding new
     dahlias and much more specific information. More
     complete and up-to-date, this is the best
     currently available dahlia guide in print.
169. Damp, Philip. GROWING DAHLIAS. London: Croom Helm,
     1981. 139p.
     Specifically focused on growing dahlias in
     England, this title would be of interest only to
     dedicated dahlia growers. Dahlia propagation,
     good cultural information, possible pests and
     diseases, and exhibiting dahlias are covered in
     detail.

## DAYLILIES (Hemerocallis)
(see publications (619-20) and quarterly (545) of the
American Hemerocallis Society)

170. Davis, Ben Arthur. DAYLILIES AND HOW TO GROW THEM.
     Atlanta: Tupper & Love, 1954. 149p.
     An older title that contains much information on

the culture of daylilies. Worth keeping but
superseded by the paperbacks published by the
American Hemerocallis Society cited above. Older
cultivars are listed here.

DELPHINIUMS
(for older pre-1970 listings see the list (597) of
the Royal Horticulture Society)

171. Edwards, Colin. DELPHINIUMS. London: Dent, 1981. 192p.
Knowledgeable cultural advice, detailed
propagation techniques, and a listing of desired
cultivars highlight this modern, well
illustrated monograph. Although oriented toward
English growing conditions, this would be the
bible for delphinium growers anywhere. An
impressive listing of delphinium species from
throughout the world was carefully compiled.

GENTIANS

172. Klaber, Doretta. GENTIANS FOR YOUR GARDEN. New York:
M. Barrows, 1964. 141p.
Gentians are well covered in this and the
following title. Mrs. Klaber was a noted American
rock garden expert, and her book abounds with
practical growing experience with these sometimes
difficult plants. She carefully defines many
species — some of which have been reclassified
since her work. This book has charm.

173. Bartlett, Mary. GENTIANS. New York: Hippocrene
Books, 1976. 160p.
An English title that combines good cultural
advice for English conditions with good
illustrations of many Gentian species.
Gentians that the author has found of ornamental
use (perennials, hybrids, and annuals) are
included. More up to date in its nomenclature,
this title should be used in conjunction with Mrs.
Klaber's more practical American title (172).

IRIS
(see also publications (621-25) and quarterly
(546) of the American Iris Society)

174. THE WORLD OF IRISES. Edited by Bee Warburton,

Melba Hamblen, assistant editor. Wichita, KS: American Iris Society, 1978. 494p.
This comprehensive title contains chapters on many aspects of this diverse genus written by over thirty iris experts from throughout the world. History, classification, culture, and lengthy discussions of iris types are included. Scholarly and exhaustive, this monograph might contain too much detail for those just seeking beginning information on iris. Good glossary, bibliographies, and index.

175. Price, Molly. THE IRIS BOOK. 2nd. ed. New York: Dover Pub., 1973. 204p.
This practical handbook is out of date, but its virtue is that it was written by an American. It is arranged by broad types of iris. Of historical interest for its cultivar recommendations and its knowledge of American growing conditions.

176. Mathew, Brian. THE IRIS. New York: Universe Books, 1981. 202p.
The classification of species of the genus Iris is described in depth in this recent monograph. Generally for each species, precise and detailed botanical descriptions are featured as well as discussions of native habitat. Cultivation information is given for those species that the author has seen grown. Brief descriptions of growing iris in general garden cultivation, water gardens, rock gardens, woodland gardens, bulb frames, pots, and greenhouses are covered. For serious iris enthusiasts this would be an important book.

177. Cassidy, G.E., and S. Linnegar. GROWING IRISES. Portland, OR: Timber Press, 1982. 160p.
The arrangement of this iris title is by the use of iris in the landscape, such as for perennial gardens, wild flower gardens, water gardens, rock gardens, or in the alpine house. Cultural information, recommended cultivars, and historical information are also covered. The authors are members of the British Iris Society so information on culture and hardiness should be translated by the reader for their own conditions.

178. Randall, Harry, IRISES. New York: Taplinger,

1969. 176p.
Iris are broadly defined and discussed by class
and variety including bulbous, Siberian, bearded,
species and others. Good cultural information
is given for different climatic conditions with
basic rules of good cultivation emphasized.
Cultivars recommended are of pre-1969 varieties.
Somewhat out-of-date but a good book on iris.

179. Dykes, William Rickatson. THE GENUS IRIS. Cambridge:
University Press, 1913. 245p.
Detailed botanical descriptions of Iris species
are given in this large sized, beautifully
illustrated monograph. It is the outstanding
watercolors that makes this title so valuable. It
was reprinted in reduced but attractive format by
Dover Press in 1974. For historical collections or
those interested in botanical illustration.

## PEONIES

(see also the publication (632-34) and quarterly
(548) of the American Peony Society)

180. Nehrling, Arno and Irene Nehrling. PEONIES OUTDOORS
AND IN. New York: Dover Pub., 1975. 288p.
An older title first published in 1960 which
contains detailed information on herbaceous and
tree peonies. Informally written, it contains
chapters on why peonies fail to bloom, peonies in
floral design, and much more detailed information.
Useful to peony specialists for its detailed
cultural information and for its listings of older
cultivars. The American Peony Society
publications cited above contain more up-to-date
information and are highly recommended.

181. Stern, Frederick Claude. A STUDY OF THE GENUS PAEONIA.
London: The Royal Horticultural Society, 1946. 155p.
This monograph is a gardening and botanical
classic which is now very expensive to purchase.
Mr. Stern enumerates the species of peony (as of
1946) in detail. Naming authority, botanical
description, and distribution are covered. The
illustrations by Lilian Snelling are among the
best examples of 20th century botanical
illustration.

PRIMROSES
(see also the quarterly (549) of the American
Primrose Society)

182. Klaber, Doretta.  PRIMROSES AND SPRING.  New York:
     M. Barrows, 1966.  125p.
     The American rock garden expert, Doretta Klaber,
     produced  a practical growing guide for the  major
     Primula  species  and   cultivars grown  in  this
     country.  Chapters on types of primroses describe
     their characteristics and give practical  cultural
     advice.  A good chapter on growing primroses from
     seed  is  included.   Practical  and  written  for
     American gardeners.
183. Clapham, Sidney.  PRIMULAS.  South Brunswick, NJ:
     A.S. Barnes, 1972.  143p.
     Outdoor  and  indoor  cultivation  of  Primula  is
     covered  in  this  good  introductory  text.   The
     species that are most often found in    successful
     cultivation  in England are included.   Basics  of
     cultivation,  propagation,  and  the selection  of
     varieties  for  specific  purposes  are  detailed.
     Greenhouse  and  alpine house culture are  briefly
     covered.  This  book  has  not  been  edited  for
     American  conditions  or  to  include  sources  of
     supply for this side of the Atlantic.
184. Hecker, W.R.  AURICULAS & PRIMROSES.  Newton Centre,
     MA: Charles T. Branford, 1971.  216p.
     The  auricula  type primroses are  generally  cool
     greenhouse  plants in England and are more  rarely
     grown in North America.  Of more interest here is
     Mr. Heckler's discussion of primroses.  They are
     of primroses commonly grown in England and so  are
     of  more  interest  to  primrose  specialists.
     Certainly  of  less  value than the title  by  the
     American, Doretta Klaber (182).


ROSES
(The  many excellent publications (636-37) and the
monthly  periodical  (554) of  the  American  Rose
Society are highly recommended.)

185. Malins, Peter, and M.M. Graff.  PETER MALINS' ROSE
     BOOK.  New York: Dodd, Mead, 1979.  258p.
     This  small-sized  book  is  one  of  the  better
     practical  guides to   growing  roses.   Planting,
     summer  care,  and pests and diseases of roses are

among the topics carefully detailed. Two common
questions on roses, pruning and the degree and
kind of care necessary in winter are well
answered. It has excellent, up-to-date (1979)
descriptions for selecting varieties of hybrid
teas, floribundas, shrubs, climbers, and historic
roses.

186. Gibson, Michael Dara. THE BOOK OF THE ROSE. New York:
      Methuen, 1980. 279p.
      A beautifully designed and illustrated English
      title on roses. The text is a combination of rose
      history, cultural advice, and the definition of
      the many rose types and hybrids. The cultural
      advice covers a broad range of growing conditions
      and is generally excellent. Major exhibition rose
      gardens throughout the world are listed and
      described. Appended are rose suppliers, a
      glossary, and bibliography. One of the most
      comprehensive manuals and also one of the most
      beautiful. The rose paintings included are by
      Donald Myall.

187. Nisbet, Fred J. GROWING BETTER ROSES. New York:
      Knopf, 1974. 253p.
      Excellent cultural advice is featured in this rose
      manual. Specifics of winter protection,
      fertilizers, mulches, pest control, pruning and
      much more are treated in depth. Unusual topics
      discussed include growing roses in the greenhouse
      and container rose growing. A good cultural
      guide.

188. Krussmann, Gerd. THE COMPLETE BOOK OF ROSES.
      Portland, OR: Timber Press, 1981. 436p.
      Inclusive, not complete, is this monumental work
      on roses presented here in translation from its
      1974 German edition. In this reference guide one
      can find fact, lore, legend, scientific studies,
      statistics, and more. One of the better sources
      on rose history, it traces roses not only in
      Europe but also in Asia, the mid-East and
      elsewhere. European rose development from the
      Middle Ages through the beginnings of modern
      hybrids is given in depth. Detailed propagation
      and hybridization information is included although
      this title should not be considered a guide to
      growing roses. The best rose reference work,

except for answering questions on practical rose culture.

189.  Browne, Roland A. THE ROSE-LOVER'S GUIDE: A PRACTICAL HANDBOOK ON ROSE GROWING. New York: Atheneum, 1983. 235p.
Practical advice on planning and planting the rose garden, the selection of roses, and the care of roses is included in this title. Asexual propagation (cuttings, budding) and the hybridizing of new roses are covered in depth. A classified listing of the pre-1974 rose hybrids that are the author's favorites is appended. A practical approach to rose gardening especially useful for those growing roses in more southern gardens.

190.  Genders, Roy. THE ROSE; A COMPLETE HANDBOOK. Indianapolis, IN: Bobbs-Merrill, 1966. 623p.
This title is one of the better rose manuals for detailed cultural information (for English gardens) and for its descriptions of many rose hybrids. Information on perfume in the rose, rose culture in greenhouses, rose recipes, and more are found here. It has a definite English bias, and is out of date, but it is more complete than many newer manuals.

191.  Thomas, Graham Stuart. THE OLD SHRUB ROSES. London: J.M. Dent/Royal Horticultural Society, 1983.
The historic roses of the past are featured in this classic rose title. The long history of these roses is traced from the early crosses that produced the gallicas, damasks, Provence, moss roses and the white roses of the past. For each of these historically important roses, information as to where and when these roses were reputed to have been introduced to cultivation and their long and interesting subsequent histories are included. This survey traces the earliest mention of these roses (some many centuries B.C.) up to present day uses.

192.  Thomas, Graham Stuart. SHRUB ROSES OF TODAY. Rev ed. London: J.M. Dent, 1980. [Dist. by Biblio Dist.]
Many species and varieties of shrub roses that have been grown in the last two centuries and not treated in the author's OLD SHRUB ROSES (191), are grouped and defined in this title. This title is divided into two broad sections, those having

an affinity to the China rose and those that do
not. Another classic study of these roses by this
influential rosarian.

193. Thomas, Graham Stuart. CLIMBING ROSES OLD AND NEW.
Rev ed. London: J.M. Dent/Royal Horticultural
Society, 1983. [Dist. by Biblio Dist.]
Climbers and ramblers (which the author
differentiates) are detailed in this English
title. Over three quarters of the text is devoted
to the description of the many historical roses
and a few of the newer introductions. This title
is of use only to dedicated rose growers as it
describes English-grown varieties, many of which
are only of historical interest. The work
includes only brief cultural information.

194. MODERN ROSES 8. Harrisburg, PA: McFarland Co.,
1980. 580p.
This title's purpose is "to serve as an
international check-list of all registered rose
names." For each listed name, information on
hybridizer, year of introduction or origination,
parentage, classification, important awards with
dates, and descriptions of shape, size, quantity,
fragrance, color, foliage, and habit of growth are
included. Appended is a listing of hybridizers
with a short address given. As the title
indicates, this is the eighth title in this
series. Older editions are in demand for
historical information on earlier introduced
roses.

195. Fitch, Charles Marden. THE COMPLETE BOOK OF
MINIATURE ROSES. New York: Hawthorn Books,
1977. 342p.
Because miniature roses require different care
than other roses, this title is very useful.
Cultural information for indoor and outdoor
culture of miniatures is given in detail. Good
photographs illustrate not only miniatures but
also their growing methods. Included with the
section on the history of miniatures is a
discussion of major contemporary hybridizers from
throughout the world. Sources for both plants and
supplies are appended.

196. Griffiths, Trevor. THE BOOK OF OLD ROSES. London:
Michael Joseph/Mermaid Books, 1984.
[Dist by Merrimack] 168p.

The many color photographs of this glossy title
help in the identification of many of the old
historic roses. Mr. Griffiths is a nuseryman in
New Zealand who specializes in these roses. The
text is divided into chapters on each of the
historic rose types. Cultural information is very
briefly given.

## VIOLETS

197. Coon, Nelson. THE COMPLETE BOOK OF VIOLETS. South
     Brunswick, NJ: A.S. Barnes, 1977. 147p.
     Written by an American expert who wrote his first
     book on violets in 1925, this book probably
     contains everything one needs to know on general
     violet culture. Violets here include outdoor
     cultivated violets, indoor Parma violets, and
     pansies. Also included is much folklore and
     historical information. This title is very
     informally written with no index, so a reader has
     to read through the text to obtain its
     considerable information.
198. Klaber, Doretta. VIOLETS OF THE UNITED STATES.
     South Brunswick, NJ: A.S. Barnes, 1976. 208p.
     This large sized, beautifully illustrated
     monograph was Mrs. Klaber's last work and
     evidences years of research. Because violet
     species are difficult to identify, this is
     primarily an identification guide for North
     America violet species with some concomitant
     growing advice. For violet enthusiasts, this is
     both an identification guide and also an example
     of somewhat stylized botanical illustration.
199. Coombs, Roy E. VIOLETS: THE HISTORY AND CULTIVATION
     OF SCENTED VIOLETS. London: Croom Helm, 1981. 142p.
     Species and hybrid violets that are cultivated in
     England are described in this modern title. Most
     of the hybrids will be hard to obtain and also to
     cultivate under most North American conditions.
     Added features are a selection of verses on
     violets and an annotated bibliography.

## Bulbs

200. Miles, Bebe. BULBS FOR THE HOME GARDENER. New York:

Grosset & Dunlap, 1976. 208p.
An attractive, carefully written title on bulbs by
an American gardener. Excellent introductory
chapters define what bulbs are, give a short
historical account of bulbs, and also discuss
basic cultural information. Two encyclopedic
sections on both hardy and tender bulbs give the
gardener necessary practical gardening advice for
each type of bulb. An important part of this
title is the carefully executed color renderings
of these plants by Judy Singer. Forcing hardy
bulbs, bulb propagation, and bulbs in the
landscape are briefly covered. Although there are
more inclusive guides to bulbs, this is the best
book on bulbs for American gardeners in terms of
coverage, its American gardening bias, and also
for its beautiful illustrations.

201. Mathew, Brian. DWARF BULBS. New York: Arco Pub.,
     1973. 240p.
     Specialists in growing more unusual bulbs will
     find in this title a wealth of information that is
     hard to obtain elsewhere. Bulbs grown in
     England in herbaceous borders, the lawn, rock
     gardens, bulb frames and in the greenhouse are
     included. Basic bulb cultivation is first
     discussed followed by a detailed encyclopedic
     section listing bulbs by genera. For many bulbs,
     cultivation requirements are given for particular
     species. It should be kept in mind that this
     title was written in England for English
     conditions. The author defines bulbs as "every
     possible shape and size of swollen storage organ
     below ground," while dwarf is defined as "plants
     growing under six inches." See also this author's
     THE LARGER BULBS (202).

202. Mathew, Brian. THE LARGER BULBS. London:
     Batsford/Royal Horticultural Society, 1978. 156p.
     Companion volume to the author's DWARF BULBS
     (201), this title follows similar format and
     depth of coverage. For instance, this coverage
     includes approximately 4 pages devoted to
     FRITILLARIA, 3 to TIGRIDIA, and 9 to GLADIOLUS.
     The emphasis is on species and not cultivars.
     Both volumes contain selected color photographs,
     line drawings, and excellent glossaries. Both of

Mr. Mathew's titles were written for the bulb
specialist.

203. Rix, Martyn and Roger Phillips. THE BULB BOOK: A
PHOTOGRAPHIC GUIDE TO OVER 800 HARDY BULBS.
London: Ward Lock, 1981. 192p.
This English title is subtitled "a photographic
guide to over 800 hardy bulbs." Clear color
photographs of many bulbs per page show
characteristics of roots, bulbs, foliage, and
flowers. The photographs picture the blooming
bulbs as if they were just dug from the garden.
Information on native habitat is given for most of
the species. Plant hardiness as defined here is
not reliable for many North American gardens. A
unique and recommended pictorial guide.

204. Reynolds, Marc, and William L. Meachem. THE COMPLETE
BOOK OF GARDEN BULBS. New York: Funk & Wagnalls,
1971. 373p.
A broadly scoped, practical manual on bulbs and
bulb gardening first published in 1967. Covering
most of the major and minor bulbs, this manual
would be an excellent introduction to the culture
of bulbs. Bulb culture in the garden under a
variety of climates and also forced for indoor
bloom are included. Among some of the more
unusual aspects of bulb culture included are bulb
culture for warmer climates, plants to plant in
conjunction with bulbs, how to care for bulbs as
cut flowers, and more. This title is
comprehensive, practical, and has a lot of
information not found in other manuals. The first
edition of this title was of more limited scope
and titled THE GARDEN BULBS OF SPRING.

205. Genders, Roy. BULBS. Indianapolis: Bobbs-Merrill,
1973. 622p.
A thorough treatment of most of the major and
minor bulbs cultivated in gardens. A prolific
English author, Mr. Genders here has compiled
much information on bulbs for specific purposes
plus a detailed encyclopedic section on bulb
genera. Appendices include planting depths,
planting and flowering times, and also the
flowering times for indoor bulbs. One of the most
complete references with a definite English bias.

206. Scheider, Alfred F. PARK'S SUCCESS WITH BULBS.
Greenwood, SC: Geo. F. Park Seed Co., 1981. 173p.

At first glance this seems to be a slight book,
but it includes a lot of brief information on
the diverse world of bulbs. It features an
encyclopedic listing of bulbs by genera with
variable quality color photographs showing flowers
and bulbs. Cultural information is concise. If
one is looking only for brief entries on many
common and uncommon bulbs, this title would be a
good choice.

\*     Thomas, Graham Stuart. PERENNIAL GARDEN PLANTS.
       Cited above as item 144.

207.   Baumgardt, John Philip. BULBS FOR SUMMER BLOOM.
       New York: Hawthorn Books, 1970. 234p.
       Mr. Baumgardt's manual is a more specialized title
       in that it focuses on summer and fall blooming
       bulbs. Four chapters treat tuberous begonia,
       gladiolus, lilies, and dahlias specifically,
       leaving other bulbs with an alphabetical, general
       listing. Winter storage of tender bulbs,
       conditioning of cut flowers, and diseases and
       pests are also topics discussed.

208.   Lawrence, Elizabeth. THE LITTLE BULBS: A TALE OF TWO
       GARDENS. New York: Criterion Books, 1957. 248p.
       This popular title follows the planting and
       enjoyment of bulbs in two gardens. The gardens
       were the author's small backyard garden in North
       Carolina and a friend's larger garden in Ohio
       (with whom the author maintained an active
       correspondence). This title is still read by
       gardeners because of its charming text which
       captures the author's excitement in growing bulbs.
       Chapters on narcissus, snowdrops and snowflakes,
       and "the first flower" capture what bulbs mean to
       most gardeners. Although gardeners can learn a
       lot about bulbs from this title, it is the
       author's prose that keeps this title alive.

\*     Crockett, James Underwood. CROCKETT'S FLOWER GARDEN.
       Cited above as item 148.

\*     Huxley, Anthony, ed. GARDEN ANNUALS AND BULBS.
       Cited above as item 155.
       Especially valuable for those looking for
       illustrations of bulbs.

209.   Wilder, Louise Beebe. ADVENTURES WITH HARDY BULBS.
       New York: Dover Pub., 1974. 363p.
       Louise Beebe Wilder was one of America's most
       famous garden authors. This title first

published in 1936 has long been popular with
generations of gardeners because of its
considerable information and because it is a joy
to read. After brief introductory chapters on
general bulb culture, major bulb genera are
described. Many species are included and are
given major garden uses. Her descriptions of
these bulbs and how they are used are taken from
the author's own personal observations. Species
entries would still be useful but cultivars and
hybrids listed are mainly of historical interest.

* Snyder, Leon C. FLOWERS FOR NORTHERN GARDENS.
  Cited above as item 154.
  Especially valuable for Northern gardeners
  interested in cultivating bulbs.

## Specific Bulbs

### CROCUS

210. Mathew, Brian. THE CROCUS: A REVISION OF THE GENUS
     CROCUS (IRIDACEAE). Portland, OR: Timber Press,
     1982. 127p.
     Mr. Mathew's technical monograph on Crocus species
     is similar in its scholarly treatment to his
     titles on bulbs (201, 202). It is a thorough
     discussion of the many species and some naturally
     occuring hybrids of CROCUS from around the world.
     It features detailed descriptions of these
     species, indications of flowering period, native
     habitat, along with very brief information on
     cultivating these species. Appended are a
     bibliography and a glossary.

211. Bowles, Eduard Augustus. A HANDBOOK OF CROCUS AND
     COLCHICUM FOR GARDENERS. Rev ed. London: Garden
     Book Club, 1955. 185p.
     A gardening classic first published in 1924 which
     has long been a standard reference to CROCUS and
     COLCHICUM. Mr. Bowles's text relates much
     practical growing knowledge of these plants. Some
     of the nomenclature is outdated, but Mr. Bowles
     captured the beauty of these bulbs in his prose.

### GLADIOLUS

212. Garrity, John Bentley. GLADIOLI FOR EVERYONE.

Newton Abbot, VT: David & Charles, 1975. 196p.
A monograph for the gladiolus specialist on
growing, propagating, and hybridizing these
popular plants on a large scale. Long lists of
pre-1975, mainly English cultivars are included.
Detailed information for specialists only.

213. Fairchild, Lee Meyer. THE COMPLETE BOOK OF THE
GLADIOLUS. New York: Farrar, Straus and Young,
1953. 243p.
Although very out of date in regard to its
description of hybrid gladiolus and some of the
recommendations for pest and disease control, it
is valuable for its discussion of American growing
practices.

## LILIES
(see also publications of the North American Lily
Society (626-31) and its quarterly (547)
periodical)

214. Rockwell, Frederick Frye; Esther C. Grayson; and
Jan de Graaf. THE COMPLETE BOOK OF LILIES.
Garden City, NY: Doubleday, 1961. 352p.
This older title has much practical gardening
information on the selection and culture of garden
lilies. It has the added advantage of being
written by two of America's best garden writers.
The selection of growing sites, planting, and care
is given in more detail than is found in recent
titles on lilies. A popular history of lilies is
included along with information on propagating and
breeding lilies. Out of date in its
recommendations of cultivars and hybrids and its
pest control recommendations, it is still a useful
title on the growing of lilies.

215. Synge, Patrick M., ed. LILIES. New York:
Batsford, 1980. 276p.
Henry John Elwes' monograph on lilies published in
1880 (with its nine supplements) is a work of
botanical art and a landmark of LILIUM taxonomy.
Mr. Synge has edited the text to update it along
with adding newly discovered species and new
illustrations. Varieties, cultivars, and hybrids
are also briefly discussed. Although primarily a
book of LILIUM taxonomy, some cultural advice is
also included. Chapters on propagation and pests

and diseases can also be found.  A monograph  for
lily specialists.
216.  de Graaff, Jan, and Edward Hyams.  LILIES.  New York:
Funk & Wagnalls, 1968.  142p.
Mr. de Graaff is one of America's most famous lily
hybridizers,  while Mr. Hyams is an English author
of gardening related titles.  This  collaboration
is  a practical manual for gardeners concentrating
on the modern lily hybrids.  Chapters on types of
hybrid  lilies  (mid-century,  aurelian,  madonna-
types,   etc.)  give   good   descriptions   and
information  on  their  hybridizers.  General
cultural  information  is  included  with  another
chapter on propagation of lilies.  Species lilies
are more selectively included.

NARCISSUS
(see  also  pubication of  the  American  Daffodil
Society  (613-18)  and  its  quarterly  (543)
periodical)

217.  Jefferson-Brown, Michael Joseph.  DAFFODILS AND
NARCISSI: A COMPLETE GUIDE TO THE NARCISSUS.
London: Faber, 1969.  224p.
A  model  detailed  monograph on daffodils  by  an
English authority  and grower.  Much information
is  given  on NARCISSUS species  and  the  defined
daffodil types.  There are seven chapters on major
daffodil  types alone.  Cultivation is considered
in depth with also chapters on hybridization,  and
pests and diseases.  While focused on English pre-
1969  hybrids,  the  author  does  consider  some
American  introductions.  A  detailed  text  that
would be of interest to all daffodil growers.

SNOWDROPS AND SNOWFLAKES

218.  Stern, Frederick Claude.  SNOWDROPS AND SNOWFLAKES: A
STUDY OF THE GENERA GALANTHUS AND LEUCOJUM.
London: The Royal Horticultural Society, 1956.  128p.
This  monograph on species of  GALANTHUS  and
LEUCOJUM is definitive.  Detailed entries on each
species  includes  botanical  description,
distribution, and much personal observation.  Many
photographs  and  drawings  help  identify  the
species.  Mr E.A. Bowles contributed two drawings

and a chapter on garden varieties of Galanthus.

## TUBEROUS BEGONIAS
(Other begonias are discussed under houseplants.)

219. Langdon, Brian. THE TUBEROUS BEGONIA. London:
     Cassell, 1969. 98p.
     THE TUBEROUS BEGONIA covers in depth the culture
     of these bulbs from raising them from seed and
     dormant tubers, the potting, watering, feeding,
     staking, and finally the storage of the tubers
     after their growing season. Although written in
     England, these instructions would be readily
     adaptable to North American conditions. It is
     well illustrated with drawings and photographs.
     English greenhouse varieties, propagation and
     hybridizing are also covered.
220. Catterall, Eric. GROWING BEGONIAS. Portland, OR:
     Timber Press, 1984. 132p.
     For its English perspective, this title would be
     of interest to begonia specialists. Covering
     mainly the cultivation of tuberous begonias in
     greenhouses, it includes information on care,
     propagation, and hybridization techniques. A
     selected variety of other begonia types are also
     included, but this title is mainly concerned with
     the indoor culture of tuberous begonias.

## TULIPS

221. Lodewijk, Tom. THE BOOK OF TULIPS. Edited by Ruth
     Buchan. New York: Vendome Press, 1979.
     [Dist. by Viking Press] 128p.
     The fascinating history of tulips is emphasized in
     this glossy title. Basic cultural advice is
     given with details on selecting varieties, how and
     when to plant, and other basic care. Excellent
     color photography of many hybrid varieties and
     illustrations that trace tulip history are an
     added bonus. A popularly focused title.
222. Hall, Alfred Daniel. THE GENUS TULIPA. London:
     The Royal Horticultural Society, 1940. 171p.
     Sir Daniel Hall's monograph on tulips has been one
     of the definitive studies on these bulbs for
     many years. The emphasis is on TULIPA species
     discussed in sections of groups and sub-groups.

Detailed descriptions, with native habitats, and brief personal growing observations are given for each species. Well illustrated with black and white photographs and forty drawings in color. Identification keys are included.

## Ornamental Grasses and Bamboo

223. Meyer, Mary Hockenberry. ORNAMENTAL GRASSES: DECORATIVE PLANTS FOR HOME AND GARDEN. New York: Scribner, 1975. 136p.
Ornamental grasses for the landscape is the subject of this valuable title. Mrs. Meyer received her master's degree from Cornell where she did research on these grasses. The author lists their use in the landscape as specimen plants, in water gardens, as ground covers and much more. A source list is appended. Well illustrated.

224. Loewer, H. Peter. GROWING AND DECORATING WITH GRASSES. New York: Walker, 1977. 128p.
This well known botanical artist has combined sensitive drawings with descriptions of these plants and their uses in the landscape. The title is organized by broad types of grasses (annuals, perennials), and also contains chapters on plants that resemble grasses (sedges, rushes, bamboo). A brief source list is appended. A popular title highlighted by its many drawings.

225. Lawson, A.H. BAMBOOS; A GARDENER'S GUIDE TO THEIR CULTIVATION IN TEMPERATE CLIMATES. New York: Taplinger Pub., 1968. 192p.
The culture of bamboo is covered in this specific title. After defining how bamboo grows, the author details soils, winter protection, propagation and general bamboo culture. The major genera and species are described giving distinguishing features of the canes, new shoots, cane sheaths, nodes, branching and leaves. Native habitat, method of propagation and uses are also included. As it was written in England, American gardeners will have to find hardiness information on these bamboo elsewhere.

226. Grounds, Roger. ORNAMENTAL GRASSES. New York: Van Nostrand Reinhold, 1981. 216p.

This ornamental grass book might be of interest
for its English perspective. Grasses grown in
England are described and their ornamental uses
listed. Chapters on large, medium, and small
grasses, bamboo, sedges, rushes, and cat-tails are
included. Color photographs of varying quality of
50 grass varieties are included. Although
realizing that some of these grasses are not hardy
in much of North America and might be difficult to
obtain, those searching for more information on
grasses might want to consult this well researched
title.

## Lawns

227.  Schery, Robert W.  A PERFECT LAWN, THE EASY WAY.
      New York: Macmillan, 1973.  294p.
      Originally entitled, THE LAWN BOOK, this book is
      one of the best   texts to introduce this topic
      to   amateurs.   Excellent,   detailed   sections
      describe preparation and the establishment of
      lawns.  Types of grasses, care, and possible
      problems are covered in depth.  Some of the
      disease and pest control recommendations are out-
      of-date, so local extension publications should be
      consulted.
228.  Voykin, Paul N.  ASK THE LAWN EXPERT.  New York:
      Macmillan, 1976.  249p.
      Written in question-and-answer format, this book
      contains  much useful information.  Use the index
      rather than try to   browse through the text.  It
      covers grasses for a wide range of  climates  and
      also covers basic lawn care well.
229.  Robey, Melvin J.  LAWNS: THE YEAR-ROUND LAWN-CARE
      HANDBOOK FOR ALL CLIMATES AND CONDITIONS, PLUS A
      SECTION ON GROUND COVERS.  New York: D. McKay,
      1977.  216p.
      Again, written in question-and-answer format, this
      title  also  includes  a brief section  on  ground
      covers.  Although there is less information given
      than in the above titles,  most questions on lawns
      could be answered by this book.

Woody Plants
(This section is divided into general woody
plants, trees, shrubs, dwarf woody plants and
vines and groundcovers. Some identification
guides are included. Those interested in either
trees or shrubs should keep the general woody
plant texts in mind).

230. Flint, Harrison L. LANDSCAPE PLANTS FOR EASTERN
NORTH AMERICA: EXCLUSIVE OF FLORIDA AND THE
IMMEDIATE GULF COAST. New York: John Wiley, 1983.
677p.
Mr. Flint's carefully researched work is one of
the most up-to-date reference works on woody
ornamentals. It is useful in the selection of
these plants for the home landscape. Here in
detailed, accurate form is information on "500
primary species and twice that number of related
species" of woody plants used in the landscape of
Eastern North America. Concise information is
given on natural and useful ranges, landscape
function, and adaptability to available summer and
winter light, wind, soil moisture, and soil pH
conditions. More details are included on seasonal
interest, problems and maintenance, and related
useful species. The listing and discussion of
each genus is most helpful in that it first lists
the most desired species (with explanations why
such are rated highly) and then gives secondary,
less desirable landscape plants in the same genus.
Thus, the gardener finds that Betula papyrifera is
a longer-lived tree in our landscapes than the
common Betula pendula. An excellent reference.
231. Dirr, Michael Albert. MANUAL OF WOODY LANDSCAPE
PLANTS: THEIR IDENTIFICATION, ORNAMENTAL
CHARACTERISTICS, CULTURE, PROPAGATION AND USES.
3rd ed. Champaign, IL: Stipes Pub., 1983. 826p.
Description of leaf, flower, fruit, bud, stem,
growing height, hardiness, growth habit, native
habitat, growing rate, texture, bark, leaf color,
diseases and pests, landscape value, common
cultivars, propagation, related species, and more
are given for most of the landscape plants
included in this practical title. Line drawings
of many plants illustrate leaf, fruit, and twig
characteristics. Some specific cultural
information is included. It would be a very
useful tool for gardeners for the selection of

woody plants for their landscape. An excellent
bibliography and glossary are included. This text
is often cited in bibliographies and is one of
most useful as well as inclusive manuals on woody
plants for the landscape.

232. Hillier, Harold C. THE HILLIER COLOUR DICTIONARY OF
TREES AND SHRUBS. New York: Van Nostrand
Reinhold, 1982. 323p.
Produced at the famous Hillier Nursery/Arboretum
in England, this pictorial encyclopedia contains
over 600 colored photographs of woody plants.
This title is especially useful in its listings of
modern cultivars. Descriptions given are brief.
Some of the plants and their cultivars included
are uncommon in North America. Another selection
tool with very good, small-sized photographs.

233. Hillier, Harold G. HILLIER'S MANUAL OF TREES &
SHRUBS. 5th ed. New York: Van Nostrand Reinhold,
1981. 576p.
This manual is one of the most exhaustive listings
of ornamental woody plants in that it includes
638 genera and over 8,000 specific plants.
Included is a short description of each plant with
its characteristics and its uses listed for the
landscape. The encyclopedic listing is divided
into sections on trees and shrubs, climbers,
conifers, and bamboo. Appended are a few lists of
plants for specific purposes. This reference
manual is best used in conjunction with other
texts, preferably those with a more North American
orientation to hardiness and common American
landscape uses.

234. Hardwicke, Denis, and Alan R. Toogood. EVERGREEN
GARDEN TREES AND SHRUBS. Edited by Anthony Huxley.
New York: Stirling Pub., 1984. 181p.
EVERGREEN GARDEN TREES AND SHRUBS is a handsome,
small guide for the identification of
ornamental evergreen plants. The colored drawings
are excellent for identification purposes. Also
included in this title are silhouette
representations of mature specimens. The text
briefly describes the 200 pictured plants.
Originally written in Denmark, this title is
translated here for English gardeners. This title
has had numerous editions.

235.  Hardwicke, Denis, and Alan R. Toogood.  DECIDUOUS
      GARDEN TREES AND SHRUBS.  Edited by Anthony Huxley.
      New York: Macmillan, 1973.   216p.
      Companion  volume  to EVERGREEN GARDEN  TREES  AND
      SHRUBS (234), this      title covers deciduous trees
      and shrubs with the same brief format.
236.  Helmer, M. Jane Coleman.  PICTORIAL LIBRARY OF
      LANDSCAPE PLANTS.  3rd ed.  Kalamazoo, MI:
      Merchants Pub., 1981.  vol 1.  343p.
      Trees,  shrubs,  groundcovers,  roses,  vines  and
      fruits  are among   the plant  material  commonly
      found in North American landscapes  illustrated in
      this   wide-ranging title.    Large-scaled  color
      photographs show the plants as they appear in  the
      landscape.   The  brief  captions  give  site  and
      pruning  requirements and use of the plants in the
      landscape.  Plant hardiness by zones is noted.  An
      expensive, yet useful, pictorial encyclopedia that
      can be used in plant selection.
  *   Graf, Alfred Byrd.  TROPICA.  Cited above as item 43.
      For  the identification of tropical  woody  plants
      this  pictorial  encyclopedia with photographs  in
      color could be useful.  Also this author's EXOTICA
      (41)  and  EXOTIC  PLANT  MANUAL  (42)  could   be
      consulted.
237.  Bloom, Adrian.  CONIFERS FOR YOUR GARDEN.  New York:
      Scribner, 1975.  147p.
      An  excellent  pictorial encyclopedia of  conifers
      illustrating their landscape characteristics.  The
      color  photography of the trees and shrubs  is  of
      good quality.  Brief descriptions of each pictured
      plant   and   concise   introductory    cultural
      information  is included.   Although  produced  in
      England,  this  title includes most conifers found
      in North American landscapes.
238.  Frederick, William Heisler.  100 GREAT GARDEN PLANTS.
      New York: Knopf, 1975.  216p.
      Landscape  architect  Bill Frederick  here  selects
      those ornamental woody plants (trees,  shrubs, and
      ground  covers) that in his judgment are not  used
      enough in Eastern North American landscapes.  Each
      plant  is evaluated for its landscape  effect  and
      illustrated  with color photographs.  A  personal
      selection but useful to those seeking more unusual
      and very effective landscape plants.

239.  McClintock, Elizabeth Mary, and Andrew T. Leiser. AN
      ANNOTATED CHECKLIST OF WOODY ORNAMENTAL PLANTS OF
      CALIFORNIA. Berkeley: Division of Agricultural
      Sciences, University of California, 1979. 134p.
      12,000 entries give "correct botanical names,
      botanical and commercial synonyms, cultivar names,
      and many of the common names used for woody
      ornamental plants of the Pacific states." This
      listing is valuable because it is difficult to
      find correct botanical names for many of the
      modern cultivars that are found in the landscape
      trade. It can also be used as an aid to cross
      reference common names to botanical names and to
      cross reference archaic nomenclature. A valuable
      reference tool for modern cultivars.
240.  [Harrison, Charles Richmond.] ORNAMENTAL CONIFERS.
      Edited by Julie Grace. Portland, OR: Timber
      Press, 1983.
      Although written in New Zealand, this encyclopedic
      listing pictures many of the conifers that are
      found in North American landscapes. There are
      also many illustrations of conifers that are
      unusual in North America. 554 good quality color
      photographs with brief descriptions help identify
      these plants.
241.  Bean, W.J. TREES AND SHRUBS HARDY IN THE BRITISH ISLES.
      8th ed. Edited by George Taylor. London: John
      Murray, 1970-80. 4 vols.
      One of the most detailed reference works on woody
      plants is this English title now in its eighth
      edition. The first edition was published from
      1914 to 1933. Detailed botanical descriptions of
      an exhaustive number of woody plant genera and
      their species are featured. Limited cultural
      information is included. For specialists only.
242.  Ouden, P. den, and B.K. Boom. MANUAL OF CULTIVATED
      CONIFERS: HARDY IN THE COLD- AND WARM-TEMPERATE
      ZONE. 3rd. ed. Boston: M. Nijhoff, 1982. 520p.
      This technical manual describes 303 species, 208
      varieties and formae, and 1935 cultivars of
      cultivated conifers. Tropical conifers are
      excluded. For each entry careful description,
      breeder or naming authority with date of
      introduction, and where cultivated is included.
      There are many black and white photographs and
      drawings. Useful to growers of unusual varieties

of conifers for identification purposes and for
correct nomenclature.

243. Spangler, Ronald L., and Jerry Ripperda. LANDSCAPE
PLANTS FOR CENTRAL AND NORTHEASTERN UNITED STATES.
Minneapolis: Burgess Pub., 1977. 506p.
Developed for college use, this guide might be
helpful in the selection of woody ornamentals for
the landscape. 350 plants are described and
identified by characteristics of habit, foliage,
flowers, and fruit. Cultural information on
hardiness, requirements of soil, and exposure to
possible pest and disease problems are covered.
Line drawings of leaves are given, but this title
is not designed as an identification guide. Of
less value than other books discussed in this
section such as Flint (230), but this title is
also much less costly. The binding is of poor
quality.

244. Council of Tree and Landscape Appraisers. GUIDE FOR
ESTABLISHING VALUES OF TREES AND OTHER PLANTS.
6th ed. Urbana, IL: International Society of
Arboriculture, 1983. 48p.
Homeowners often need an evaluation of the
monetary value of woody plants in their
landscapes. This brief guide helps to arrive at
evaluations based on both replacement and a "basic
formula" method. Both methods are carefully
explained in the text. Discussions of casualty
claims are also included. The preface states "the
appraiser must be a professional plantsman"
amongst other qualifications.

245. Snyder, Leon C. TREES AND SHRUBS FOR NORTHERN GARDENS.
Minneapolis: University of Minnesota Press,
1980. 411p.
Gardeners looking for woody plants that will
withstand more rigorous climates will find Dr.
Snyder's text (which was written for Minnesota's
climatic conditions) very helpful. A long
encyclopedic section which includes over 400
trees, shrubs, and vines is arranged
alphabetically by genus. The entries give
description, hardiness, culture, and use. Many
small color photographs help in identification.
Lists of plants for specific purposes are found in
a section on plant selection. General culture of
these plants is discussed briefly.

246.  Courtright, Gordon.  TREES AND SHRUBS FOR TEMPERATE
      CLIMATES.  Rev. ed. Beaverton, OR:  Timber Press,
      1984.  239p.
         Woody ornamentals grown ornamentally in California
         and other    Pacific coast states are featured in
         this pictorial guide.  Most of the  colored
         photographs  picture how these plants look in  the
         landscape  and  so  are not generally  useful  for
         identification purposes.  The plants are arranged
         by growing height.  Other reference works on woody
         plants should  be consulted in  conjunction  with
         this  title  as many of the  botanical  names  are
         incorrect.  Previously titled TREES AND SHRUBS FOR
         WESTERN GARDENS.
247.  GARDENING TREES & SHRUBS.  Birmingham, AL: Oxmoor
      House, 1980.  260p.
         A  popularly  written and excellently  illustrated
         guide  to the    woody plants suitable for use  in
         Southern gardens.  Information on planting,  care
         and  selection  for these   landscape  plants  is
         included.  The  listings are divided into  ground
         covers, vines, shrubs, and small and large trees.
248.  Perry, Bob.  TREES AND SHRUBS FOR DRY CALIFORNIA
      LANDSCAPES: PLANTS FOR WATER CONSERVATION: AN
      INTRODUCTION TO MORE THAN 360 CALIFORNIA NATIVE AND
      INTRODUCED PLANTS WHICH SURVIVE WITH LIMITED WATER.
      San Dimas, CA: Land Design Pub., 1981.  184p.
         An  example  of a regional guide to  woody  plants
         useful in a limited climatic region.  360 native
         Californian  and introduced plants were chosen for
         their adaptability to dry conditions and for their
         effective  use  in landscapes.  Over 500  color
         photographs help  identify these  plants,  and
         numerous  lists  aid  in the  selection of  woody
         plants for different locations and purposes.
249.  Lenz, Lee W., and John Dourley.  CALIFORNIA NATIVE
      TREES & SHRUBS: FOR GARDEN & ENVIRONMENT.
      Claremont, CA: Rancho Santa Ana Botanic Garden,
      1981.  232p.
         After  first  defining major plant communities  of
         southern  California  and  their  environmental
         considerations,  this  regional guide discusses  a
         selection  of native species the authors find  of
         possible  ornamental  use.  Nontechnical  but
         thorough  descriptions,  native  habitat,  and
         landscape  use are included.  Line  drawings  and

color photographs aid in identifying these plants.
A planting list for seven climatic regions and an
excellent glossary are appended.

## Trees

250. Wyman, Donald. TREES FOR AMERICAN GARDENS. Rev. and
enl. ed. New York: Macmillan, 1965. 502p.
An older title that has been the standard
reference on ornamental trees for many years.
Dr. Wyman's listing of trees by genera shows much
first hand knowledge of the growth habit and uses
of these ornamentals. It is still useful
especially for its listings of trees for specific
purposes. Lists of blooming characteristics,
foliage, fruit, order of bloom, and trees for
highway plantings are but a few of Dr. Wyman's
listings. His discussion of recommended trees
evidences much practical observation. Also
included is the 1961 American Forestry Association
file of 355 Big Tree Champions. Somewhat
superseded by Flint's title on woody plants (230).

251. Hudak, Joseph. TREES FOR EVERY PURPOSE. New York:
McGraw-Hill, 1980. 229p.
This title is a useful selection tool covering 257
trees found in North American landscapes.
Because it covers a wide range of climatic zones
(2 to 10) it is necessarily more selective, but it
therefore has a wider appeal to gardeners
throughout most of North America. Descriptions,
hardiness, ornamental characteristics, possible
problems, and common cultivars are covered.
Silhouettes of a 10-year-old specimen and a 25-
year-old specimen for each tree are included
(showing gardeners the maturing specimens) with
drawings of leaf and fruiting characteristics.
Listings of plants for specific purposes are
appended.

252. PLANTS THAT MERIT ATTENTION: VOLUME I - TREES.
Edited by Janet Meakin Poor. Portland: OR: Timber
Press/The Garden Club of America, 1984. n.p.
PLANTS THAT MERIT ATTENTION promises to be a most
valuable series for the selection of plants for
North American gardeners. This first volume
defines 143 species of trees that the Horticulture

Committee of the Garden Club of America considers
to be unfairly neglected in North American
landscapes. For each tree outstanding color
photographs show habit and closeup views of
foliage, fruit and flowering characteristics. The
text includes hardiness, good descriptions, brief
cultural information including transplanting,
propagation, and possible disease and pest
information, an evaluation of each tree's
landscape potential, and U.S. public gardens and
arboreta where these trees can be seen. Appended
are addresses of public gardens and arboreta, and
an invaluable source list with addresses of
commercial firms which sell the included trees.
Trees are also grouped by many site and habit
characteristics for selection purposes. Other
volumes on other landscape and gardening plant
materials are promised in this series. This title
is highly recommended.

253.   Lancaster, Roy. TREES FOR YOUR GARDEN. New York:
       Scribner, 1975. 146p.
       This pictorial encyclopedia of landscape trees is
       arranged alphabetically by genus. Excellent color
       photographs illustrate how these trees appear
       in the landscape or show details of their
       ornamental characteristics. The brief text
       describes why they are effective in landscapes and
       relates short histories of many. Lists of trees
       for specific purposes are found throughout the
       text.

254.   Zion, Robert L. TREES FOR ARCHITECTURE AND THE
       LANDSCAPE. New York: Reinhold, 1968. 284p.
       Focusing on trees as landscape elements, this
       large-sized title is useful as a guide for
       selecting trees for the landscape. Excellent full
       page black and white photographs picture how the
       selected trees (about 100) will look in the
       landscape at their maturity. Practical
       information is given on tree care and selection
       for landscape purposes. Design data for these
       trees are also given focusing on design
       characteristics, hardiness, ease of transplanting,
       and special requirements. A state by state list
       enumerates trees for many landscape purposes
       throughout the continental United States. There
       was a condensed edition published by the same

publisher in 1979.
255. Menninger, Edwin A. FLOWERING TREES OF THE WORLD FOR
     TROPICS AND WARM CLIMATE. New York: Hearthside
     Press, 1962. 336p.
     Covering tropical and subtropical areas, this work
     serves as a general reference guide. Native
     habitats, brief descriptions, and landscape and
     economic uses of about 500 ornamental tree species
     are included. Over 400 small, variable quality,
     color photographs are included. Because of
     incorrect names, nomenclature should be checked in
     other reference works.
256. Edlin, Herbert, and Maurice Nimmo. THE ILLUSTRATED
     ENCYCLOPEDIA OF TREES: TIMBERS AND FORESTS OF THE
     WORLD. New York: Harmony, 1978. 256p.
     One of the more complete tree encyclopedias, this
     work covers trees found worldwide. The title can
     be used as a reference guide and a pictorial
     identification guide for many of the world's
     trees. Besides the many chapters on conifers,
     deciduous and tropical trees, there are
     introductory essays on timber, the strength of
     woods, how woods are used in crafts and more.
     Colored illustrations include both drawings and
     photographs to make this title enjoyable to browse
     through.
257. Johnson, Hugh. THE INTERNATIONAL BOOK OF TREES; A
     GUIDE AND TRIBUTE TO THE TREES OF OUR FORESTS AND
     GARDENS. New York: Simon and Schuster, 1973. 288p.
     Although not as useful for identification purposes
     as Edlin (256), this popular encyclopedia is
     handsomely illustrated and informative. Botany of
     trees, historical information, and using trees in
     landscapes are some of the subjects included.
     Again as in Edlin, the chapters on specific types
     of trees are quite thorough with much specific
     information. This reference manual would have
     been of more value with a more detailed subject
     index.
258. Phillips, Roger. TREES OF NORTH AMERICA AND EUROPE.
     New York: Random House, 1978. 224p.
     This English title is a photographic
     identification guide to more than 500 common
     trees of North America and Europe. Photographs of
     leaf, fruit, flower, and bark, along with
     silhouette drawings of adult growth habit help in

identification. The photographs are in color and
identify many common trees found in North America.
This guide includes many cultivars not found in
most identification manuals.

259. Symonds, George Wellington Dillingham. THE TREE
IDENTIFICATION BOOK: A NEW METHOD FOR THE PRACTICAL
IDENTIFICATION AND RECOGNITION OF TREES. New York:
M. Barrows, 1958. 134p.
An older title that is helpful in the
identification of common trees in Eastern North
America. Photographs of leaves, twigs, flowers,
fruit, bark, and growth habit provide help for
easy identification. This title helps identify
130 native and introduced species. Biased toward
Eastern North American trees. Symonds' title on
shrubs (274) has similar format.

260. Buckley, A.R. TREES AND SHRUBS OF THE DOMINION
ARBORETUM. Ottawa: Agriculture Canada, Research
Branch, 1980. Publication #1697. 237p.
Divided into two broad sections, deciduous woody
plants and conifers, this title lists those
ornamentals that have been successfully grown at
the Dominion Arboretum. The purpose of this title
is to give an evaluation of their hardiness and
landscape effectiveness. Each section is arranged
alphabetically by genus. For species entries
among the information listed are common names,
hardiness, and descriptions of the plants giving
ornamental characteristics. Many cultivars are
listed. There are black and white and color
photographs and a hardiness zone map.

261. Hightshoe, Gary L. NATIVE TREES FOR URBAN AND RURAL
AMERICA: A PLANTING DESIGN MANUAL FOR ENVIRONMENTAL
DESIGNERS. Ames: Iowa State University Research
Foundation, 1978.
Specifically designed for use in Northeastern
United States, this attractively designed manual
has some unusual features. It is broadly divided
into an "elimination key" which lists native trees
by design characteristics, and an illustrated
section featuring drawings showing each tree's
landscape effect and identification
characteristics. 122 native plants are included.
The format and treatment of this text and its
illustrations are unusual. Maps are included to
show native habitat.

262. Blombery, Alec, and Tony Rodd. AN INFORMATIVE,
     PRACTICAL GUIDE TO PALMS OF THE WORLD. London:
     Angus & Robertson, 1982. [Dist. by Merrimack
     Pub.]. 199p.
     Since there are few nontechnical titles on palms,
     this title written is recommended for the amateur.
     It is useful for its brief cultural information
     and also for its many color photographs that make
     it a good identification guide. Major palm genera
     with their more common species are described in
     nontechnical language and given habitat, use, and
     cultivation information. Appended are listings of
     major palm collections throughout the world, lists
     of palms for specific purposes, a glossary, and a
     good bibliography.
263. McCurrach, James C. PALMS OF THE WORLD. New York:
     Harper, 1960. 290p.
     Palms are described and pictured alphabetically by
     140 genera in this landmark study. Variable
     quality black-and-white photographs help
     identify specimens. Detailed descriptions are
     included with specific cultural information.
     Added chapters include general cultural
     information, a necessary well-illustrated
     glossary, and a listing of where specimens could
     be found growing outdoors (as of 1960) in botanic
     gardens throughout the tropical world.
     Supplemented by (264).
264. Langlois, Arthur C. SUPPLEMENT TO PALMS OF THE WORLD.
     Gainesville: University Presses of Florida, 1976.
     252p.
     A companion volume to McCurrach (263), this title
     lists over 100 genera not listed in the
     previous study. The arrangement of this text is
     similar to McCurrach's title. The black-and-white
     photographs (admittedly palms are difficult to
     photograph) are again variable. The descriptions
     of genera have more depth than the original
     volume.


                              HEMLOCK


265. Swartley, John C. THE CULTIVATED HEMLOCKS. Revised
     by Humphrey L. Welch. Portland, OR: Timber Press,
     1984. 186p.

A detailed monograph on the many cultivars of
hemlock grown in North America and England.
This title began as a thesis prepared by Dr.
Swartley in 1939. After many years of work Dr.
Swartley's manuscript was finally edited and
revised by the noted English authority on dwarf
woody plants, Humphrey L. Welch. The myriad
cultivars of TSUGA CANADENSIS (Canadian hemlock)
are carefully described giving detailed
identification features and the history of their
cultivation. Other species of TSUGA and their
cultivars are also discussed. Among other topics
discussed are the economic uses of hemlock, how to
use them in the landscape, and the propagation,
diseases, and pests of these woody plants. This
is one of the most comprehensive monographs on a
single woody plant genus that is oriented toward
the amateur.

## MAGNOLIAS

266. Treseder, Neil G. MAGNOLIAS. London: Faber,
published in collaboration with the Royal
Horticultural Society, 1978. 243p.
There are few technical monographs of trees that
are of interest to home gardeners, but perhaps
this is an exception. This title discusses the
many species and hybrid magnolias with detailed
descriptions, native habitat, history, and
bibliographic citations. For hybrid magnolias,
detailed hybridization records and evaluations are
included. Cultural information is included by the
English author which can be translated to specific
North American conditions. This monograph
probably contains more information than most
gardeners would want to know about these trees.

## MAPLES

267. Vertrees, J.D. JAPANESE MAPLES: MOMIJI AND KAEDE.
Forest Grove, OR: Timber Press, 1978. 178p.
One is certainly impressed by the detail of this
beautifully produced monograph. Hundreds of
the cultivars of ACER PALMATUM and ACER JAPONICUM
(plus a few others) are pictured and described.
Historical information, culture, propagation, and

taxonomy is detailed. The photography is
excellent and good for identification purposes. A
book for the specialist.


## Shrubs

268. Wyman, Donald. SHRUBS AND VINES FOR AMERICAN GARDENS.
Rev. and enl ed. New York: Macmillan, 1969. 613p.
Dr. Wyman's title has been the standard work on
landscape shrubs and vines for many years, and
although it is somewhat outdated, it is still
recommended. Stressing species and cultivars
useful in the landscape, it includes most
information that gardeners would be seeking on how
to select, plant, and maintain these plants.
Lists compiled to help in the selection of plant
material include information on order of bloom,
ornamental fruiting characteristics, foliage
color, and much more. There are over 1,700
species and cultivars included in this useful
manual. This title is as useful for its coverage
of vines as for shrubs.

269. Hudak, Joseph. SHRUBS IN THE LANDSCAPE.
New York: McGraw-Hill, 1984. 291p.
Describing 285 species and hundreds of cultivars
of shrubs, this title is similar in intent to the
author's excellent book on trees (251). As a
selection guide, the text divides shrubs into
detailed sections on needle evergreen, broadleaf
evergreen and deciduous types. Personal
observation is evidenced in the description of
growth habit and landscape effectiveness for each
shrub. The illustrations are too small to be of
much value. Basic design principles and
cultivation techniques are briefly introduced.
Appended are lists of shrubs for specific
purposes.

270. Zucker, Isabel. FLOWERING SHRUBS. Princeton, NJ:
Van Nostrand, 1966. 380p.
An older title that still is very useful.
Covering hardiness zones 1 to 6, it contains
information on 579 shrubs and 117 small trees
useful as ornamental plants in these zones.
Although entries are short, landscape use is
stressed and personal observations noted.
Flowering characteristics are illustrated with

photographs. Lists of shrubs for specific
purposes and a chart of blooming dates are also
included.

271. Crockett, James Underwood. FLOWERING SHRUBS. The
Time-Life Encyclopedia of Gardening. Alexandria,
VA: Time-Life, 1972. 160p.
Brief descriptions arranged by genera of many of
the most ornamental shrubs are included in this
title. The information includes descriptions of
the most common species, cultivars, or hybrids and
brief growing instructions. The color drawings
show flowering and fruiting characteristics and
general growth habit. The introductory chapters
are similar to other volumes in this series in
that they contain pictorial essays giving ideas on
what shrubs can be used for in the landscape.

272. Gault, Simpson Millar. THE COLOR DICTIONARY OF SHRUBS.
New York: Crown Pub., 1976. 208p.
Over 500 color photographs of cultivated shrubs
commonly grown in England are pictured and
described in this attractive title. Although this
title mainly illustrates species, it also pictures
some hybrids (over 30 Rhododendron hybrids are
included). The text describes each pictured shrub
and its use in the landscape. Written in England,
this title contains plants like Abutilon and
Fuchsia which are not commonly defined as shrubs
in this country.

273. Hellyer, Arthur G.L. GARDEN SHRUBS. London: Dent,
1982. 248p.
A selected listing of the shrubs commonly grown in
England is the feature of this up-to-date manual.
Arranged by genera, this 273-shrub listing
contains general descriptions, growing height and
width, flower color, and information in coded form
on foliage characteristics, hardiness (for English
conditions), pruning instructions, and
propagation. A few line drawings and color
photographs are included. General discussions on
shrubs detail general care, pests and diseases,
and pruning among other topics. Appended are
lists of plants for special purposes and a
bibliography. Abutilon, Fuchsia, and tree peonies
are among the plants described that are not
usually found in North American shrub manuals.

This title is of interest only to experienced gardeners.

274. Symonds, George Wellington Dillingham. THE SHRUB IDENTIFICATION BOOK: THE VISUAL METHOD FOR THE PRACTICAL IDENTIFICATION OF SHRUBS, INCLUDING WOODY VINES AND GROUND COVERS. New York: M. Barrows, 1963. 213p.
Similar in treatment to this author's identification manual on trees (259), this title identifies many of the native and cultivated shrubs through pictorial keys. Among the identifying details featured are thorns, leaves, flowers, fruit, twigs, and bark. Again the bias of this title is toward shrubs grown in the eastern United States.

275. Sherk, Lawrence C., and A.R. Buckley. ORNAMENTAL SHRUBS FOR CANADA. Ottawa: Canada Department of Agriculture, Research Branch, 1968. Publication # 1286. 187p.
This government publication focuses on the shrubs suitable for use in the wide-ranging climatic conditions of Canada. It is mainly a listing of these plants by genus. Generic listings include general description and indications of why each is valued in the landscape. Species entries give height, hardiness, common names, and their value in the landscape. There are numerous variable quality color and black and white photographs. Also included is brief information of general culture, pruning, diseases, and pests of shrubs. Lists of shrubs for specific purposes and hardiness zone maps are also included. Also published in French under the title, ARBUSTES ORNEMENTAUX POUR LE CANADA.

CAMELLIAS
(see also the publications (604) and quarterly (541) of the American Camellia Society)

276. Noble, Mary, and Blanche Graham. YOU CAN GROW CAMELLIAS. New York: Dover Pub., 1976. 257p.
Written for American gardeners, this practical guide has very good cultural information on the growing of camellias in the South and under cover in less temperate conditions. Watering, fertilizing, pruning, mulching, disbudding,

propagation and possible pests and diseases are
covered in detail. Added features of the text
include a brief history of camellia cultivation,
major species and hybrids (as of 1962),
landscaping with camellias, gardens throughout the
world which feature these plants, and a glossary.
Comprehensive and useful for its cultural advice,
this is one of the better guides to these popular
plants.

277. Macoboy, Stirling. THE COLOUR DICTIONARY OF CAMELLIAS.
Sydney: Lansdowne Press, 1981. 208p.
Carefully reproduced color photographs of many of
the historically important and universally
popular cultivars of camellia are featured in this
handsome photographic guide. Arranged by camellia
type there are chapters on CAMELLIA JAPONICA, many
of the Asiatic cultivars, miniatures, fragrant
varieties, and even some of the related genera of
plants. The text is historically orientated and
gives introduction dates and some descriptive
information. This guide is useful for its
considerable historical information and as an
identification guide.

278. Durrant, Tom. THE CAMELLIA STORY. Auckland, NZ:
Heinemann, 1982. [Dist. by ISBS] 159p.
Again historical information on camellias
predominates in this text with only one short
chapter on the culture of camellias in climates
similar to New Zealand's. The photography is
outstanding but more selective than in Macoboy's
title (277). Appended are addresses of camellia
societies and a bibliography.

279. Chang, Hung Ta, and Bruce Bartholomew. CAMELLIAS.
Portland, OR: Timber Press, 1984. 211p.
For camellia specialists, this taxonomic guide to
the CAMELLIA is an up-to-date description of about
200 species. Many of the species are unknown
outside of Asia. Detailed botanical descriptions
are included along with 74 line drawings. This
text was translated and edited from the 1981
Chinese edition by Mr. Bartholomew. Of limited
appeal.

## HEATHS AND HEATHERS

280. Underhill, Terry L. HEATHS AND HEATHERS: CALLUNA,

DABOECIA AND ERICA. New York: Drake Pub.,
1972. 256p.
The genera CALLUNA, DABOECIA and ERICA are
included in this small, practical guide on the the
selection, planting, and care of these plants,
which are more popular in Europe. The description
of species and the many cultivars of these plants
is outstanding. It would be useful for American
gardeners to consult American authorities, such as
Everett (38) to find out which varieties are
cultivated in North America and how they are
grown. Among the appended materials in this text
are a blooming calendar and a glossary.

281. Laar, Harry van de. THE HEATHER GARDEN: DESIGN,
MANAGEMENT, PROPAGATION, CULTIVARS. London:
Collins, 1978. 160p.
The use of heathers in the landscape, good
cultural advice, and concise descriptions of many
species and cultivars are included in this text
originally published in Holland in 1974. Numerous
color photographs and line drawings are included.
Proper soils, pruning, winter protection,
propagation, and pests and diseases are some of
the topics discussed. Also included are a key to
species and hybrids of Calluna and Erica, a
glossary, and a short bibliography.

282. Proudley, Brian, and Valerie Proudley. HEATHERS IN
COLOUR. New York: Sterling Pub./Blandford Press,
1974. 192p.
This small-sized title is useful as an
identification guide for heathers as it contains
over 100 color photographs of many species and
cultivars. The brief text includes general
cultural information for climates similar to
England's.

LAUREL

283. Jaynes, Richard A. THE LAUREL BOOK: REDISCOVERY OF
THE NORTH AMERICAN LAURELS. New York: Hafner
Press, 1975. 180p.
An excellent monograph on the many native and
cultivated laurel (KALMIA) of North America.
Detailed descriptions, black and white and color
photographs, line drawings, and cultural
information are included. Although of limited
interest, this is an excellent work on one genus

presented in a nontechnical style.

## LILACS

284.  THE EDWARD A. UPTON SCRAPBOOKS OF LILAC INFORMATION.
[S.l.]: International Lilac Society, 1980.
Mr. Upton, who died in 1959, maintained a clipping
file on lilacs and at his death they were
presented to Arnold Arboretum in Massachusetts.
Volumes 1 and 2 are reprinted here in one large
paperback and contain much information of variable
quality on the culture and description of species
and older cultivars. Each volume has a limited
index. For lilac specialists only.

285.  McKelvey, Susan Delano. THE LILAC; A MONOGRAPH.
New York: Macmillan, 1928. 581p.
This classic monograph on lilacs is still one of
the best works available on these popular shrubs.
Its detailed enumeration of lilac species and
early cultivars fills 500 pages. Culture,
propagation, insects and pests, and historical
data are also included. Although dated in
nomenclature and cultivars, it certainly should be
consulted for those seeking detailed information
on these plants.

## RHODODENDRONS
(see also the quarterly (551) of the American
Rhododendron Society)

286.  Leach, David G. RHODODENDRONS OF THE WORLD AND HOW
TO GROW THEM. New York: Scribner, 1961. 544p.
An older title, but still one of the best
monographs on this genus. Especially valuable are
chapters on rhododendrons for landscape use, for
less temperate climates, and for cool greenhouses.
Mr. Leach details the planting and subsequent care
of rhododendrons describing proper soils, mulches,
winter protection, disbudding, pruning, and
fertilizing. His discussions of species and
hybrids while somewhat out of date, still form an
exhaustive listing as of 1962. This title is
still in demand by rhododendron specialists.

287.  Greer, Harold E. GREER'S GUIDE TO AVAILABLE
RHODODENDRONS: SPECIES & HYBRIDS. Eugene, OR:

Offshoot Pub., 1982. 151p.
While the culture of rhododendrons is briefly covered, the main feature of this title is its listing and evaluation of species and hybrids. For each entry a lengthy description is given with height, hardiness, season of bloom, and a quality rating of flowering, general appearance, and landscape performance included. A useful listing of species that has different rhododendron classification systems is appended. The color photographs are of good quality. This title is especially useful for those living in climates similar to the Pacific Northwest.

288. Cox, Peter Alfred. DWARF RHODODENDRONS. New York: Macmillan, 1973. 296p.
This title and its companion volume (289) on species of RHODODENDRON should be consulted by anyone seeking detailed information. The species descriptions include naming authority, habit, flowering characteristics, native habitat, and evaluations for cultivation purposes. Also included are detailed information on propagation, garden uses, cultural information, and pests and diseases. Listings giving species for woodland gardens, late flowering varieties, ratings by color, and many other characteristics are given.

289. Cox, Peter Alfred. THE LARGER SPECIES OF RHODODENDRON. London: Batsford, 1979. 352p.
Companion to this author's DWARF RHODODENDRONS (288), this volume contains discussions of RHODODENDRON over five feet. It is similar in scope and treatment.

290. American Rhododendron Society. AMERICAN RHODODENRON HYBRIDS. Edited by Meldon Kraxberger. Tigard, OR: author, 1980. 244p.
A detailed description, history, and help in the selection of hybrid rhododendron is the feature of this title. The hybrid listing is alphabetical giving rating, hardiness, height, blooming date, parentage, date of introduction, and description of leaves and flowers. A historical section traces the hybridization of rhododendrons in six regions of the United States. Also listed are award winning hybrids. 20 American Rhododendron Society chapters from throughout the United States have also compiled helpful selection lists of

         those hybrids that do well in their regions.
291.  Galle, Fred C.  AZALEAS.  Birmingham, AL: Oxmoor
      House, 1974.  96p.
      The cultivation of rhododendrons in the South is
      described in this handsomely produced title.  The
      climatic area of the South covered in this
      title ranges from zones 6 through 9.  Excellent
      recommendations of azalea hybrids are given along
      with detailed cultural information.  Two other
      sections describe azalea display gardens of the
      South and recommend companion plants to grow with
      azaleas.
292.  Davidian, H.H.  THE RHODODENDRON SPECIES: LEPIDOTES.
      Portland, OR: Timber Press, 1982.  vol 1.  431p.
      For specialists on RHODODENDRON this currently
      published series would be very valuable.  It
      provides technical descriptions of all species,
      subspecies and varieties recognized by Mr.
      Davidian.  The first volume contains Lepidote
      RHODODENDRON (those with scales on branches,
      leaves or flowers).  Besides the exhaustive
      descriptive information, also included are naming
      authority, history, indication of native country,
      relative hardiness, and flowering dates.
293.  HYBRIDS AND HYBRIDIZERS, RHODODENDRONS AND AZALEAS
      FOR EASTERN NORTH AMERICA.  Edited by Philip A.
      Livingston and Franklin H. West.  Newtown Square,
      PA: Harrowood Books, 1978.  256p.
      Detailed chapters on five major Eastern
      hybridizers highlight this text for rhododendron
      specialists.  Also of interest are detailed
      listings of ratings and recommendations of hybrids
      for various Eastern North American conditions.
      The five hybridizers included are Charles Owen
      Dexter, Joseph Benson Gable, Benjamin Yeo
      Morrison, G. Guy Nearing, and Anthony M.
      Shammarello.

                       Dwarf Woody Plants

294.  Wyman, Donald.  DWARF SHRUBS; MAINTENANCE FREE WOODY
      PLANTS FOR TODAY'S GARDEN.  New York: Macmillan,
      1974.  140p.
      DWARF SHRUBS is a small book that offers
      practical advice on dwarf plants for gardeners.
      The encyclopedic section is arranged by genus and
      lists commonly grown species, and their growing

heights, common names, hardiness, and nontechnical descriptions. As in Dr. Wyman's other woody plant titles, his lists of plants for specific purposes are very useful for purposes of plant selection. For instance, dwarf shrubs are listed by flowering, fruit and foliage color, for dry soils, seashore planting, and many other selection criteria. The color photographs included are too small to be of much worth. This book includes both deciduous and evergreen plants.

295. Keith, Rebecca McIntosh, and F.A. GILES. DWARF SHRUBS FOR THE MIDWEST. Urbana: Univerisity of Illinois Press, 1980. 163p.

Over 100 shrubs generally under four feet of height are included in this practical title. Landscape use is discussed as well as general cultivation requirements. For each shrub, description of growth habit and hardiness is included. Photographs and line drawings of growth habit, and leaf, flowering, or fruiting characteristics help identify these plants. Plants included in this title are appropriate for plant hardiness zones of two to six.

296. Welch, H.J. DWARF CONIFERS, A COMPLETE GUIDE. Newton, MA: C.T. Blandford, 1966. 334p.

Dwarf conifers grown in England are both described and given good cultivation information. The cultural information is for English conditions. The conifers are discussed by genus and list many cultivars, subspecies, varieties, and forms. The shrubs are described in nontechnical terminology. Of special merit are the numerous black and white photographs including a number of identification keys showing foliage characteristics.

297. Hornibook, Murray. DWARF AND SLOW-GROWING CONIFERS. 2d. ed. Sakonnet, RI: Theophrastus, 1973. 286p.

This classic English text's second edition first published in 1938, is still in demand because of its considerable information. Chapters on specific genera describe many of the varieties, subspecies, forms and cultivars giving bud, branch, and leaf characteristics. Most of these shrubs are very rare, therefore this title is for dwarf woody plant connoisseurs.

## Ground Cover Plants and Vines

298.  Wyman, Donald. GROUND COVER PLANTS. 5th. ed.
      New York: Macmillan, 1970. 175p.
      Low perennials, shrubs, and vines which spread
      rapidly and keep close to the ground are discussed
      here.   Dr. Wyman limits his discussion of plants
      to those shorter than three feet. For the 250
      described    plants,    flowering    and    foliage
      characteristics,    height,    native   habitat,
      propagation, and landscape use are included. As
      usual in Dr. Wyman's titles, the lists detailing
      ground covers for many specific purposes are
      useful   selection   tools.   There are more recent
      titles on ground covers available from England;
      however, these plants do not adapt themselves to
      North American conditions. This makes Dr. Wyman's
      text still highly recommended.

299.  Thomas, Graham Stuart. PLANTS FOR GROUND-COVER.
      Rev ed. London: J.M. Dent, 1983. [Dist. by
      Biblio Dist.]
      Listing the considerably more numerous plants used
      in England as    ground covers, this title would
      be of interest to the more experienced gardener or
      plantsman.  Mr.  Thomas divides his discussion of
      these   plants   into   shrubs,   climbing   plants,
      conifers,   herbaceous plants,   ferns, grasses, and
      rushes.   In each section, country of origin,
      height, planting distances, leaf color, indication
      of  whether deciduous or evergreen,  flower height
      and    color,    flowering    season,    habit,    and
      propagation  method are included.  This  text  is
      comprehensive and well arranged.   It is of less
      value than Dr. Wyman's title (298) only because of
      its  bias  toward English cultural practices and
      plant material.

## VINES
(see also ivy under house plants)

*     Wyman, Donald. SHRUBS AND VINES FOR AMERICAN GARDENS.
      Cited above as item 268.

300.  Cravens, Richard H. VINES. The Time-Life
      Encyclopedia of Gardening. Alexandria, VA:
      Time-Life Books, 1979. 160p.
      This valuable introduction to vines focuses  both
      on  the  identification  of  common vines and  the

uses of these vines in the landscape. The
encyclopedic listing of vines by genera includes
good colored drawings to help identify them. The
introductory essays might give gardeners ideas for
using vines in their landscape. Vines included
are perennial, annual, and tropical vines.

301. Brilmayer, Bernice. ALL ABOUT VINES AND HANGING
PLANTS FOR INTERIOR DECORATION, IN THE LANDSCAPE,
IN CONTAINER GARDENING. Garden City, NY: Doubleday,
1962. 384p.
Mrs. Brilmayer's text covers vines for outdoor,
indoor, and container culture. Her comprehensive
listing of vines is arranged alphabetically by
genus. Thus Cissus (discussed as a houseplant) is
found next to Clematis. Good general discussions
are included on landscape use of vines, their use
as houseplants, how to propagate vines, and
possible problems with vines. This title is out-
of-date in cultivar and hybrid selection, and its
bibliography and source list.

302. Menninger, Edwin A. FLOWERING VINES OF THE WORLD.
New York: Hearthside Press, 1970. 410p.
Especially valuable for its listing of vines from
tropical and subtropical areas of the world, this
encyclopedia describes 2,000 vines with 600
photographs. Most entries include nontechnical
descriptions of the vines with common names and
indications as to where the vines are cultivated.
Many authorities on different plant families
contributed to this volume.

303. Beckett, Kenneth A. CLIMBING PLANTS. Portland, OR:
Timber Press, 1983. 178p.
Although written in England, the text also
considers North American growing conditions. Its
main feature is an alphabetical listing of vines
by genus. Decriptions are nontechnical in manner
with the vine's ornamental uses included. General
cultural information is also included. Appended
are lists of vines for specific purposes, rated by
hardiness, for walls, listings by flower color,
etc.

304. [Harrison, Richmond E.] CLIMBERS AND TRAILERS.
Edited by Jane Grace. Wellington, NZ: A.H. &
A.W. Reed, 1983.
Clear color photographs of over 250 of the
tropical and subtropical vines of the world are
featured in this photographic encyclopedia.

Although clematis, sweet peas, ivy, and climbing
roses are found here, it is the listing of the
more uncommon vines (DREGEA, CAVENDISHIA,
CORONILLA) that makes this text valuable. The
picture captions give brief nontechnical
descriptions of the vines and how they are used.

305.  Rose, Peter Q. CLIMBERS AND WALL PLANTS: INCLUDING
      CLEMATIS, ROSES AND WISTERIA. Poole, Dorset:
      Blandford Press, 1982. [Dist. by Sterling Pub] 168p.
      This English title includes those plants that the
      author considers of ornamental value as climbers
      and as wall plants. Wall plants include such
      plant material as the tree peony, mockorange, and
      forsythia, all plants that can be trained or
      espaliered on a wall. The author describes each
      plant giving a short history of the plant, its
      ornamental uses, and indications of where it is
      grown (including some information on North
      American conditions). It is an informal book that
      gardeners might enjoy reading.

## CLEMATIS

306.  Lloyd, Christopher. CLEMATIS. London: Collins,
      1977. 208p.
      This excellent monograph defines the species and
      hybrids of clematis that have ornamental uses.
      Mr. Lloyd divides his discussion of hybrids by
      flower color and divides his discussion of species
      into groups such as viticellas and montanas. The
      considerable cultural information is given for
      English conditions, so gardeners might need to
      consult other sources for their less temperate
      climatic conditions. Excellent advice is given on
      pruning and training types of clematis. The color
      illustrations are by the famous botanical artist,
      Marjorie Blamey. This title is one of the best
      single genus monographs even though it was not
      written with North American gardeners in mind.

307.  Fisk, Jim. THE QUEEN OF CLIMBERS. Suffolk: Fisk's
      Clematis Nursery, 1975. 88p.
      This guide is written by an English nurseryman who
      has specialized in clematis. It is informally
      written for English gardeners. Mr. Fisk's
      practical experience in clematis culture and his
      rating of the merits of the many clematis hybrids
      and species are what most American gardeners will

find of use. His earlier book on clematis was
SUCCESS WITH CLEMATIS.

## Vegetables

308. Crockett, James Underwood. CROCKETT'S VICTORY GARDEN.
Boston: Little, Brown, 1977. 326p.
Deservedly popular, the late Mr. Crockett's
practical gardening manual contains much more than
just information on vegetable gardening. Also
included is information on perennials, annuals,
houseplants and other gardening topics. Vegetable
garden preparation, step by step instructions on
growing vegetables from seed to harvest, and good
discussions of the pests and diseases of
vegetables are all covered. Because it is written
in calendar format, its excellent index should be
consulted often since basic care of common
vegetables is spread over many chapters. Lushly
illustrated.

309. Abraham, George. THE GREEN THUMB BOOK OF FRUIT AND
VEGETABLE GARDENING. Englewood Cliffs, NJ:
Prentice-Hll, 1970. 355p.
This is one of the most practical vegetable
gardening manuals and is also useful as a guide to
tree and small fruit culture. Pruning grapes,
planting asparagus, growing hickories,
strawberries and much, much more are included.
Written from practical experience it is a good all
in one vegetable and fruit manual. However, some
of the pest and disease control recommendations
are out-dated.

310. Seymour, John. THE SELF SUFFICIENT GARDENER: A
COMPLETE GUIDE TO GROWING AND PRESERVING ALL YOUR
OWN FOOD. Garden City, NY: Doubleday, 1979. 256p.
This comprehensive manual attractively presents
information on starting vegetable and fruit
gardens, selecting which types of produce the
gardener should include, and how to preserve this
produce for year around use. The deep bed method
of intensive gardening is introduced along with
other basics of garden planning. This title is
attractively produced with good drawings
illustrating both specific garden vegetables and
fruits along with basic gardening processes. It
emphasizes natural methods of pest and disease
control. Although written in England it is also

well suited for North American gardeners. A
contemporary title which presents its material in
an attractive manner.

311.  Bartholomew, Mel. SQUARE FOOT GARDENING. Emmaus, PA:
Rodale Press, 1981. 347p.
Intensive vegetable gardening practices (growing
more in less space) are described in depth in this
title. Special planting bed preparation,
suggestions on spacing of plants, successive
plantings, structures for vertical vegetable
growing, construction of cages to protect plants
from pests and inclement weather, and ways to
extend the growing season are all covered. A very
practical title.

312.  Faust, Joan Lee. THE NEW YORK TIMES BOOK OF
VEGETABLE GARDENING. New York: Quadrangle/New
York Times Book Co., 1975. 282p.
Well written and more complete than many vegetable
gardening titles, this guide includes basic
planning and planting information on vegetable
gardens, the cultivation of specific vegetables
(also 12 herbs), and general vegetable care. A
novice gardener should find most basic questions
on vegetables and their care answered here.

313.  GROWING VEGETABLE & HERBS; WITH RECIPES FOR THE
FRESH HARVEST. Birmingham, AL: Oxmoor House,
1984. 272p.
The practicalities of designing, constructing,
planting, and maintaining vegetable and herb
gardens in most Southern growing conditions are
detailed in this handsome manual. Discussions of
specific vegetables and herbs include practical
growing tips, harvesting information, recommended
varieties and even recipes focusing on the
specific vegetables. Beautifully illustrated and
designed, this is one of the better gardening
books for the South.

314.  McNeilan, Ray A. PACIFIC NORTHWEST GUIDE TO HOME
GARDENING. Portland, OR: Timber Press, 1982. 302p.
The specifics of vegetable gardening, small fruit,
and tree fruit culture for conditions in
Northwestern North America are covered in this
practical title. Informally written, it provides
detailed information on many aspects of food
production.

315.  Esmonde-White, Anstace. VEGETABLE GARDENING. Toronto:
McGraw-Hill Ryerson, 1981. 192p.

Although written specifically for Canadian gardeners, this title is one of the better guides to vegetable gardening. The author takes the gardener through many practical steps, from sharpening gardening tools to descriptions of soil preparation to the actual planning and planting of a vegetable garden. Her description and information on specific garden vegetables is listed by family. The author more briefly also covers herbs and the cultivation of fruit. A good vegetable gardening manual, especially for northern gardeners.

316.  Burrage, Albert Cameron.  BURRAGE ON VEGETABLES.
      Revised by Susan A. Hollander and Timothy K.
      Hollander. Boston: Houghton Mifflin, 1975.  224p.
      This text has the most detailed description of the cultivation of specific vegetables of any vegetable gardening manual. It also features evaluations of recommended varieties of these vegetables. Mr. Burrage's rating system of vegetables is unique (and controversial!) giving asparagus, for instance, 100 and the lowly cucumber with 20. Cooking instructions for the vegetables are also included. While this title is entertaining to read, it also contains much practical information. Recommended for those who specialize in vegetable gardening.

## TOMATOES

317.  Hendrickson, Robert.  THE GREAT TOMATO BOOK: THE ONE
      COMPLETE GUIDE TO GROWING AND USING TOMATOES
      EVERYWHERE. New York: Stein and Day, 1984.  226p.
      For those fixated on this vegetable, here is a guide to everything one could want to know about tomatoes. The book's 226 pages cover not only information on many varieties but culture by every conceivable method and conserving and using tomatoes. A good title devoted solely to this special vegetable.

## GOURDS

318.  Heiser, Charles Bixler.  THE GOURD BOOK.  Norman, OK:
      University of Oklahoma Press, 1979.  248p.
      The history, lore, and practical uses of this wide-ranging group of plants are the focus

here. Topics range from decorative uses to
anthropological evidence of the use of gourds.
There is one short section on gourd culture.
Although this is a technical study, those seeking
information on gourds will want to consult this
title.

## Herbs

319. Foster, Gertrude B., and Rosemary F. Louden. PARK'S
     SUCCESS WITH HERBS. Greenwood, SC: G. W. Park
     Seed Co., 1980. 192p.
        Certainly one of the great book values is this
     handy, practical guide to these useful plants.
     More than 100 kinds of herbs are included. Each
     herb is pictured in small color photographs,
     described, and given growing instructions. Also
     practical suggestions for the use of these plants
     are included. Mrs. Foster and her daughter are
     both recognized experts on herbs and their
     practical knowledge is demonstrated throughout the
     text. An unusual and useful feature of this title
     are the small color photographs that identify
     herbs in their young seedling stage. This title
     is highly recommended for any collection on herbs.
320. Loewenfeld, Claire, and Philippa Back. THE COMPLETE
     BOOK OF HERBS AND SPICES. New York: Putnam,
     1974. 313p.
        Over 100 herbs and spices are described in detail
     by these English authors. Each herb entry includes
     plant description, native habitat, cultivation,
     harvesting, storing, uses, and even recipes.
     Handsomely illustrated with colored and black and
     white drawings, this title also makes a good
     identification guide. Color illustrations are
     omitted in paperback editions.
321. Swanson, Faith H., and Virginia B. Rady. HERB GARDEN
     DESIGN. Hanover, NH: University Press of New
     England, 1984. 155p.
        This unique book on the design of herb gardens
     illustrates the process of planning and
     constructing such a garden. The authors give more
     than fifty sample plans ranging from the simplest
     beginner's gardens to large-scaled elaborate
     public gardens. The details of the executed plans
     (indications of paving materials, the

differentiation of the plant materials, even the
ornamental north points) are outstanding. The
text follows this high standard as it carefully
explains the creative process and the installation
of a herb garden. The authors ingeniously carry
the gardener through this planning process into
the actual construction of a herb garden. They
illustrate how, because of site limitations and
personal preferences, changes had to be made in
the original plan. One of the best of recent
gardening titles.

322. Clarkson, Rosetta E. HERBS, THEIR CULTURE AND USES.
New York: Macmillan, 1972. 226p.
This title has long been a favorite with herb
gardeners. Basics of herb cultivation,
propagation, uses, harvesting, and storing are
included. One third of the book is a tabular
compilation of 101 useful herbs. 26 other tables
list herbs for specific purposes. This older
title is still one of the better texts on herbs.

323. Simmons, Adelma Grenier. HERB GARDENING IN FIVE
SEASONS. New York: Van Nostrand, 1964. 353p.
Adelma Simmons has been an influential American
herb grower and author for many years. Among
her many books on herbs is this title which takes
the herb gardener through the seasons with herbs.
Informally written, it discusses planning the herb
garden, care and use of many individual herbs, and
harvesting and includes some recipes using herbs.
There is a dictionary of fifty selected herbs with
line drawings, description, and cultivation.
Appended are lists for herbs for specific purposes
and a pronounciation guide.

324. Elbert, Virginie F., and George A. Elbert. FUN WITH
GROWING HERBS INDOORS. New York: Crown Pub.,
1974. 192p.
The authors have practical experience in the
growing of these plants indoors, and they
succinctly impart the basics of indoor herb
cultivation. It is questionable if it really is
as easy to grow these plants indoors as the
authors maintain. Well illustrated and written.
Sources of herbs and supplies are appended.

325. Simon, James E.; Alena F. Chadwick; and Lyle E. Craker.
HERBS: AN INDEXED BIBLIOGRAPHY 1971-1980. Hamden,
CT: Archon Books/Shoe String Press, 1984. 770p.
Researchers seeking detailed information on herbs

and many related subject classifications will find
this bibliography helpful.  For each major herb,
there    is    descriptive    information    on    plant
chemistry, botany, horticulture, pharmacology, and
use.    The    bibliographic references on each    herb
are then listed.    These citations are given    full
treatment    in    a    listing    arranged    by    subject.
Finally    there    are    lists    of    herb    books,
bibliographies,    reports    of    conferences    and
symposia,  and general references.  There are also
author and subject indexes.

326.   Rohde, Eleanour Sinclair.  HERBS AND HERB GARDENING.
       Detroit: Gale Research, 1976.
       Eleanour Rohde was a recognized English    authority
       on herbs.    This title is her most practical guide
       for    beginners,  but most beginners will    want    to
       reading    her    book in conjunction with other    more
       recent herb manuals.    Her prose does capture "the
       charm  of herb gardens" which is the title of    her
       first chapter.

327.   Sanecki, Kay Naylor.  THE COMPLETE BOOK OF HERBS.
       New York: Macmillan, 1974.  247p.
       This English title is divided into three sections:
       a history, herbs in cooking, and a practical guide
       to cultivation and use.    Practical information is
       combined  with  excerpts from  the  literature  of
       earlier writers on herb plants.    Many recipes are
       included in the culinary section.    Common names of
       herbs in English,  French,  German,  Spanish,    and
       Italian are appended.

328.   Garland, Sarah.  THE COMPLETE BOOK OF HERBS & SPICES.
       New York: Viking Press, 1979.  288p.
       Good    illustrations  for  identification  purposes
       along    with    recipes    for using herbs    highlight
       this    handsome    title.    Besides    the    culinary
       recipes,  there  are  recipes for  natural  insect
       repellents,  washing  and  polishing concoctions,
       cosmetics,    incense,    candle    making,    dyes,    and
       medicinal    purposes.    There are nearly 300    herbs
       and spices included,    making this a good reference
       guide.

329.   Andrews, Theodora; William L. Corya; and Donald A.
       Stickel, Jr.  A BIBLIOGRAPHY ON HERBS, HERBAL
       MEDICINE, "NATURAL" FOODS, AND UNCONVENTIONAL
       MEDICAL TREATMENT.  Littleton, CO: Libraries
       Unlimited, 1982.  339p.
       This    topically    annotated    bibliography    gives

selective listings on many broad aspects of herbs
and herb growing. Chapter headings include herb
growing, cooking, medicinal plants, wild plants
and foraging, poisonous plants, folk medicine, and
more. The annotations are critical. A more
detailed and technically oriented herb
bibliography is listed above (325).

330. Lewis, Walter H., and Memory P.F. Lewis. MEDICAL
     BOTANY: PLANTS AFFECTING MAN'S HEALTH. New York:
     John Wiley, 1977. 515p.
     This title should be consulted by those seeking
     more scientific and authoritative information
     on medicinal plants. It is divided into three
     broad sections on injurious plants, remedial
     plants, and psychoactive plants. Active
     components, how the plants are used, and some
     historical information is included for each listed
     plant. Many charts, illustrations, and references
     are features of this study.

331. ENCYCLOPEDIA OF HERBS AND HERBALISM. Edited by
     Malcolm Stuart. New York: Grosset & Dunlap,
     1979. 304p.
     A reference section on 420 herbs with
     illustrations, descriptions, cultivation, constit-
     uents, and use is the main portion of this book.
     There are also chapters on history, the practical
     uses of herbs, and a general chapter on
     cultivation, collection, and preservation of
     herbs. There are indexes to plants and general
     subjects.

332. MEDICINES FROM THE EARTH: A GUIDE TO HEALING PLANTS.
     Edited by William A.R. Thomson. New York:
     McGraw-Hill, 1978. 208p.
     Useful both for its good illustrations and
     reference information, this popular guide to
     medicinal plants is also one of the most complete
     (247 plants are included). Listings of plant
     remedies for common ailments, the history of folk
     plant medicine, and instructions for harvesting
     and preparing teas, compresses, and salves are
     included. A general index would have been
     helpful.

333. Boxer, Arabella, and Philippa Back. THE HERB BOOK.
     New York: Octopus/Mayflower, 1980. 224p.
     This is a combination of a coffee-table-type book
     and a practical manual. Included are
     descriptions of 50 popular herbs and the uses of

these herbs medicinally, in cosmetics, and for cooking. There are recipes in all three sections. As the authors are English, the recipes are given in both American and metric measurements.

334.  HERBS AND SPICES: THE PURSUIT OF FLAVOR. Edited by Waverly Root. New York: McGraw-Hill, 1980. 191p. "The pursuit of flavor" is the focus of this guide to culinary herbs and spices. Recipes, historical information, and their use throughout the world are included. 100 plants are included.

335.  Grieve, Maud. A MODERN HERBAL; THE MEDICINAL, CULINARY, COSMETIC AND ECONOMIC PROPERTIES, CULTIVATION AND FOLK-LORE OF HERBS, GRASSES...New York: Dover Pub., 1971. 2 vols. 888p. A compilation of the "useful" properties of 800 kinds of herbs is featured in this classic study written in 1931. Excerpts from earlier writers on herbs are featured. This title is out of date and therefore should not be used as a practical guide to medicinal plants, but it is of use as a source of lore and historical information on herbs.

336.  Lesch, Alma. VEGETABLE DYEING; 151 COLOR RECIPES FOR DYEING YARNS AND FABRICS WITH NATURAL MATERIALS. New York: Watson-Guptill, 1970. 146p. Both methods and specific recipes are given for natural plant dyeing in this practical title. Good descriptions of equipment needed, the processes of collecting, preserving dye materials, and sources of supply are given. Two appended charts give information on dye substances and color information in tabular form. No illustrations.

337.  Grae, Ida. NATURE'S COLORS; DYES FROM PLANTS. New York: Macmillan, 1974. 229p. Basics and specifics on plant dyeing using lichens, wildflowers, weeds, garden flowers, shrubs, trees, and food related plants are included. Recipes are easy to follow and relatively specific. The text includes good illustrations of plants with color photographs of some sample dyed products.

338.  Casselman, Karen Leigh. CRAFT OF THE DYER: COLOUR FROM PLANTS AND LICHENS OF THE NORTHEAST. Toronto: U. of Toronto Press, 1980. 249p. While oriented toward the plants and lichens that are found in  the Northeast, this text is also a good  introduction to the process of using natural

dyes. Dyeing procedures, equipment, mordants,
dyestuffs, and natural fibers are all well
discussed. The section on specific plants and
lichens occupies over two thirds of the book and
is arranged according to common name. Parts used,
processing procedures, colors obtained, fastness,
availability, and identifying features are listed
for each plant. A good reference.


Fruits & Berries

339. Hill, Lewis. FRUITS AND BERRIES FOR THE HOME
     GARDEN. Charlotte, VT: Garden Way Pub., 1980? 269p.
     Much practical experience is evidenced in this
     title on tree fruits, nuts, bramble fruits,
     strawberries, and grapes. Good basic advice on
     fruit culture is given (for instance, see dwarf
     fruit trees or grape pruning). Disease and pest
     problems are not minimized as in many popular
     fruit manuals. It includes advice for those who
     spray as well as for organic gardeners. This
     title has good information presented in a concise
     manner.
340. Hendrickson, Robert. THE BERRY BOOK:THE ILLUSTRATED
     HOME GARDENER'S GUIDE TO GROWING AND USING OVER 50
     KINDS AND 500 VARIETIES OF BERRIES. Garden City,
     NY: Doubleday, 1981. 259p.
     Strawberry, blueberry, cranberry, huckleberry,
     elderberry, blackberry, boysenberry, dewberry,
     raspberry, gooseberry, currant, and mulberry are
     some of the edibles covered in this title.
     Although information is detailed, this title would
     best be used in conjunction with county extension
     publications for local cultural needs. A few
     errors are evident such as recommending
     controlling spider mites with malathion.
     Preparation of planting areas, specific cultural
     information, control of diseases and pests, and
     even recipes are included.
341. Weaver, Robert John. GRAPE GROWING. New York:
     Wiley, 1976. 321p.
     Although this is a college-level textbook, this
     title would be useful for those looking for more
     technical information on grapes than can be

found in general fruit texts or gardening
encyclopedias. Detailed information on grape
varieties (as of 1976), propagation, culture,
pruning, training, harvesting, and pests and
diseases are included. A brief history of the
culture of grapes is given along with a short
account of how to make wine at home. This work
contains a good glossary, bibliography, and index.

342.  Bultitude, John. APPLES: A GUIDE TO THE
      IDENTIFICATION OF INTERNATIONAL VARIETIES.
      Seattle, University of Washington Press, 1983. 325p.
      Apple varieties from Europe, North America, South
      Africa, Australia, and New Zealand are identified
      and described in this manual. 252 apples are
      described and pictured in both black and white and
      color photographs. The color photographs show
      apples as they are attached to branches while the
      black and white photographs show cross sections of
      the fruit. History, fruiting season, synonyms,
      references, and descriptions of the trees,
      flowering, and fruit color, shape, size, etc., are
      included in the text. Attempts to be inclusive
      but the Winesap apple, for one, is not found.

343.  Brooks, Reid M., and H.P. Olmo. REGISTER OF NEW
      FRUIT AND NUT VARIETIES. 2d ed. Berkeley:
      University of California Press, 1972. 708p.
      The 3,847 varieties of fruits and nuts introduced
      in the United States and Canada between 1920 and
      1970 are described in this valuable reference
      manual. Topically arranged under common names of
      the fruits and nuts (from almonds to walnuts),
      each entry includes originator, date of
      introduction, description of fruit and tree,
      season, and other useful information. Appended is
      a listing of patented varieties and an index.

344.  Swenson, Allan A. LANDSCAPE YOU CAN EAT. New York:
      McKay, 1977. 211p.
      An apt title that describes the approach of this
      book for the homeowner. Although basics are
      covered, not enough detailed information is
      included on the many edible plants discribed.

345.  Tukey, Harold Bradford. DWARFED FRUIT TREES FOR ORCHARD
      GARDEN, AND HOME...WITH SPECIAL REFERENCE TO THE
      CONTROL OF TREE SIZE AND FRUITING IN COMMERCIAL FRUIT
      PRODUCTION. Ithaca, NY: Cornell U. Press, 1978. 562p.
      Written for both amateur gardeners and professional

fruit growers, this classic monograph has not been bettered. It was first written in 1964 so some of the material is out dated. Espalier, bracing and trellising, growing fruit under glass, as bonsai, and much more are included. The basics of tree structure, stock-scion relationships, and other aspects of dwarf fruit tree culture are also covered.

## Nuts

346.  NUT TREE CULTURE IN NORTH AMERICA. Edited by
      Richard A. Jaynes. Rev. ed. Hamden, CT:
      Northern Nut Growers Association, 1979. 466p.
      This revised handbook on nut trees covers most common and uncommon nut varieties. Although chapters are written by different specialists, the coverage is generally uniform. Nuts suitable for most climatic regions are covered, but many tropical varieties (for instance, cocoa or coconuts) are omitted. For those interested in tropical nut crops see Menninger (347). Those consulting this work will need to use the excellent index. Local extension publications should be used to decide which varieties can be grown in specific climatic regions. The 1969 edition was published under the title of HANDBOOK OF NORTH AMERICAN NUT TREES.

347.  Menninger, Edwin Arnold. EDIBLE NUTS OF THE WORLD.
      Stuart, FL: Horticultural Books, 1977. 175p.
      More useful as a reference manual than a practical growing guide, this title contains much information on the worldwide culture of nuts, fruits, and seeds. It is especially useful for information on species grown in tropical areas. Black and white photographs of variable quality help in identification.

348.  Rosengarten, Frederic, Jr. THE BOOK OF EDIBLE NUTS.
      New York: Walker, 1984. 384p.
      THE BOOK OF EDIBLE NUTS is a reasonably inclusive reference to 42 different types of commonly cultivated nuts. Their history, lore, and harvesting techniques are discussed. Cultivation information is not included. Recipes are featured.

*     Brooks, Reid M. REGISTER OF NEW FRUIT & NUT VARIETIES.
      Cited above as item 343.

## Houseplants

349.  SUCCESS WITH HOUSE PLANTS.  Pleasantville, NY:
      Reader's Digest, 1979.  480p.
      Many have found this manual to be one of the most
      useful texts on houseplant culture because of the
      detailed information it provides.  It covers the
      basics on indoor culture well and includes most of
      the plants one should attempt to grow indoors all
      in great detail.  For instance, in a section on
      watering one finds out how, how often, and why one
      should water as recommended.  How to water
      plentifully, moderately or sparingly (not easy to
      generalize about) is explained in this text.
      Filled with clear and colorful illustrations and
      accurate cultural information, this attractive
      houseplant manual is highly recommended.

350.  Crockett, James Underwood.  CROCKETT'S INDOOR GARDEN.
      Boston:  Little, Brown, 1978.  325p.
      Arranged month-by-month through the indoor
      calendar gardening year, this title copies the
      format of Crockett's very successful book on
      vegetables (308).  This title is not designed as a
      reference tool as it is to be read through month-
      by-month, so information on specific subjects is
      scattered throughout the text.  As one might
      expect from a title developed after many years of
      television involvement, this book is handsomely
      illustrated with many color photographs.

351.  Fitch, Charles Marden.  THE COMPLETE BOOK OF
      HOUSEPLANTS.  New York: Hawthorn Books, 1972.  308p.
      Described as containing information on over 1000
      house plants, this title has proven to be one of
      the better guides to their culture.  Mr. Fitch is
      a careful writer and has researched his manual
      well.  Basics of house plant culture (watering,
      propagating, potting, etc.) are well defined.  Mr.
      Fitch is also a well-known plant photographer, so
      his illustrations are of good quality.  A good
      beginner's manual that has enough detail to prove
      useful.

  *   Graf, Alfred Byrd.  EXOTICA.  Cited above as item 41.
      For identification of tropical plants this
      pictorial encyclopedia is excellent.  Mr. Graf's
      two other titles, TROPICA (43) and the EXOTIC
      PLANT MANUAL (42) are also useful.

352.  THE COLOR HANDBOOK OF HOUSE PLANTS.  Edited by Elvin
      McDonald, Jacqueline Heriteau, and Francesca Morris.
      New York: Hawthorn Books/Wentworth Press, 1975.  256p.
      For brief information on specific houseplants  and
      for  its  short  discussion  of  general  houseplant
      culture, this title has much to recommend it.  For
      250  houseplants,  general growth  characteristics
      are  described  along with their requirements  for
      light,   temperature,   soil,   watering,   feeding,
      possible   problems,   desired   containers,   and
      propagation.  A commonsense,  brief treatment  of
      the culture of these plants.
353.  Mott, Russell C.  THE TOTAL BOOK OF HOUSE PLANTS.
      New York: Delacorte Press, 1975.  208p.
      The  colorful  plant  paintings of  this  handsome
      encyclopedia of indoor plants makes identification
      easy.  Cultural  information on these  plants  is
      also  covered well.  Including 350 indoor plants,
      this title should answer many questions of  indoor
      gardeners.
354.  RODALE'S ENCYCLOPEDIA OF INDOOR GARDENING.  Edited by
      Anne M. Halpin.  Emmaus, PA: Rodale Press,
      1980.  902p.
      Information on soils,  plant foods,  forcing bulbs
      indoors,  and  terrariums  are contained in  this
      indoor gardening title.  The focus is on  indoor
      gardening not just growing houseplants.  Published
      by  Rodale  Press,  it  stresses the  benefits  of
      organic gardening methods indoors.  Those looking
      for  more  than capsule  information  on  specific
      houseplants  should  look  elsewhere,  but  basic
      information  on  such  broad subjects  as  bonsai,
      growing   herbs   indoors,   and   greenhouses   is
      included.
355.  Faust, Joan Lee.  THE NEW YORK TIMES BOOK OF HOUSE
      PLANTS.  New York: Quadrangle Books, 1973.  274p.
      This  general  houseplant  manual  has  more
      information  included  than   many  titles   on
      houseplants.  Over  100 specific houseplants  are
      described in capsule form.  Small colored drawings
      help in their identification.  While this title is
      a  good beginner's  guide,  more  experienced
      gardeners  looking  for detailed information  will
      need to consult other works.
356.  Elbert, George, and Virginie Elbert.  PLANTS THAT
      REALLY BLOOM INDOORS.  New York: Simon & Schuster,
      1974.  222p.
      An  optimistic  title,  but gardeners  have  to  be

optimistic!    Flowering tropicals of all  types
are described,  illustrated,  and  provided  with
specific  growing  information.   Some of the  more
exotic varieties may be hard to grow and purchase,
but  locating them is made easier with the list of
sources appended.   The authors seem very familiar
with  the  many exotics  they  describe.   Another
title by the Elbert's (324), details growing herbs
indoors,  while  another highlights the  gesneriad
family (357).

357.  Elbert, Virginie, and George Elbert.  THE MIRACLE
      HOUSEPLANTS: THE GESNERIAD FAMILY.  New and enl. ed.
      New York: Crown, 1984.  272p.
      The  gesneriad  family contains many of  the  most
      popular  flowering houseplants (african  violets,
      streptocarpus,  gloxinias,  episcias).   This  new
      edition,  with  its  updated nomenclature and  new
      cultivars,  is  an excellent introduction  to  the
      wide  variety of plants in this family and to  the
      very  diverse  cultural  requirements  of  these
      plants.    Well  illustrated  for  identification
      purposes  and  with  detailed,  specific  cultural
      information (soil mediums, temperatures, light and
      humidity  requirements,  watering,  and fertilizer
      requirements),  this is one of the best titles  on
      the culture of indoor plants.

358.  Hay, Roy; F.R. McQuown; and G.K. Beckett.  THE
      DICTIONARY OF HOUSE PLANTS.  New York: McGraw-Hill,
      1974.  224p.
      500  color  photographs of many indoor plants  are
      the focus of this   identification manual.   Each
      plant  is  also described and recommended care  is
      given in capsule form.  Produced in England.

359.  Titchmarsh, Alan.  THE LAROUSSE GUIDE TO HOUSE PLANTS.
      New York: Larousse, 1982.  286p.
      Featuring  350 colored drawings of indoor  plants,
      this  recent  title  is  a  useful  identification
      manual.   Written in England, it covers most of the
      more  common  indoor plants  arranged  by  family.
      This   arrangement  brings  plants  with   similar
      characteristics  together,  making  identification
      easier.  The cultural information included is very
      brief.

360.  Loewer, H. Peter.  BRINGING THE OUTDOORS IN: HOW TO
      DO WONDERS WITH VINES, WILDFLOWERS, FERNS, MOSSES,
      BULBS, CACTI, AND DOZENS OF OTHER PLANTS MOST
      PEOPLE OVERLOOK.  New York: Walker, 1974.  168p.

Covering a wide range of topics on indoor gardening, this title is more than another houseplant manual. The author is well known as a plant illustrator and his drawings here are among his best. His interest in this title is in both growing unusual plants indoors and growing plants in unusual ways. Hanging gardens, terrariums, wild flowers indoors, and insectivorous plants are a few of his unusual topics. A handsome title and an unusual title.

361. Kramer, Jack. AN ILLUSTRATED GUIDE TO FLOWERING HOUSEPLANTS: HOW TO ENJOY YEAR-ROUND COLOUR IN YOUR HOME, FEATURING 150 PLANTS. New York: Routledge Press, 1981. 160p.

One of America's most prolific authors, Mr. Kramer sometimes produces a useful title. This houseplant manual would be a good beginner's guide for both identification purposes with its color photographs and also for its brief cultural information. It was previously published as GROWING BEAUTIFUL FLOWERS INDOORS. Only for those looking for the briefest of information.

AFRICAN VIOLETS

(see also the gesneriad society publications for african violets (571-73) ).

362. Free, Montague. ALL ABOUT AFRICAN VIOLETS: THE COMPLETE GUIDE TO SUCCESS WITH SAINTPAULIAS. Edited by Charles Marden Fitch. Rev ed. Garden City, NY: Doubleday, 1979. 255p.

"America's favorite house plant" is thoroughly examined in this revised handbook. Cultural details on potting, soils, proper growing conditions, and watering are covered in depth. Recent developments in new hybrids and violet forms are included. The many problems with these plants are sanely discussed. First published in 1949, the book has been updated with new photographs by Mr. Fitch. Although a source list is appended, ordering from suppliers advertising in the gesneriad and african violet journals could bring better results.

363. Robey, Melvin J. AFRICAN VIOLETS, QUEENS OF THE INDOOR GARDENING KINGDOM. San Diego: A.S. Barnes, 1982. 199p.

Another good title on the culture of these plants

but less attractive and up-to-date than the
Free/Fitch title (362). The cultural information
and information on african violet problems is,
however, complete. A straightforward presenta-
tion.

## AMARYLLIS

364. Traub, Hamilton Paul. THE AMARYLLIS MANUAL.
New York: Macmillan, 1958. 338p.
A title that should answer any questions on
amaryllis. A detailed discussion of amaryllis
species and cultivars is followed by information
on culture, breeding, and propagation. More
information is included than all but the most
dedicated amaryllis fanciers need to know.
Written by a recognized expert on the amaryllis
family, this title is outdated in its naming of
cultivars but has not been superseded.

## BEGONIA
(see also tuberous begonia under bulbs (219-20),
and the bimonthly (560) of the American Begonia
Society.)

365. Thompson, Mildred L., and Edward J. Thompson.
BEGONIAS. New York: Times Books, 1981. 356p.
One of the best monographs on specific
houseplants, this is a compendium of knowledge
on begonias accumulated over a long period by
these begonia enthusiasts. Large scaled in every
respect, this volume contains an exhaustive
descriptive listing of begonias classified by
broad begonia type. General and specific cultural
information for these diverse plants is
excellently presented. The many color and black
and white photographs aid in identification.
Other aspects of begonia growing such as
propagation and hybridizing are covered in depth.
A model popular monograph attractively produced.
It was updated by the authors with a supplement in
1984.
366. Misano, Isamu. BEGONIAS. Japan: Bunka Shuppab-sha,
1974. 237p.
367. BEGONIAS. Los Angeles: American Begonia Society,
1978. [translation] 77p.
An identification manual containing about 300

color    photographs      of begonias.    A companion
volume   published by The American Begonia   Society
gives   a translation of the Japanese   text.    This
translation describes the varieties pictured   with
information     on     history     and    identification
characteristics.     Both  volumes   are    available
through the American Begonia Society.

368.  BEGONIAS.  Toyko: Seibundo Shikosha Pub., 1980.  222p.
Numerous  color photographs of begonias make   this
paperback useful for identification purposes.   The
text  is in Japanese,  but the    photographs  are
identified by botanical Latin.  For specialists.

369.  Brilmayer, Bernice.  ALL ABOUT BEGONIAS.
Garden City, NY: Doubleday, 1960.  223p.
Certainly  the  best guide to begonias before  the
Thompsons' manual    (365) was written, this title
still  has  worth  for  begonia  fanciers.   Good
growing  information  is combined with  a  limited
description of begonia species and cultivars as of
1960.

BROMELIADS
(see also the quarterly (564) and the publications
(638-41) of The Bromeliad Society.)

370.  Rauh, Werner.  BROMELIADS FOR HOME, GARDEN AND
GREENHOUSE.  Poole: Blandford Press, 1979.  431p.
First published in German in 1970-73, this  title
was translated and is now recognized as one of the
most  complete  references to these plants.   It is
divided into two sections,  growth and culture and
a description of genera and species.   This  title
is  less  valuable  as a guide  to  growing  these
plants  than  as a reference to the many  species.
In   its   generic  listing  detailed   botanical
identification characteristics  are  given   with
naming authorities, synonyms, native habitats, and
culture.   Many  black  and white photographs  and
line  drawings  help in  identification.   A  good
reference tool.

371.  Kramer, Jack.  BROMELIADS.  New York: Harper & Row,
1981.  179p.
Although  this prolific author has  written  other
books on bromeliads, this book is by far his best.
Well    illustrated with both color and black and
white photographs, it can be useful in identifying
these  diverse  plants.   Cultural  information  is

both general for bromeliads and also specific for
different genera. This cultural information is
brief yet to the point. Kramer convinces one that
he is interested in and knows these plants.

372. Benzing, David H. THE BIOLOGY OF THE BROMELIADS.
Eureka, CA: Mad River Press, 1980. 305p.
Written for the bromeliad specialist, this manual
contains the most detailed information in
monograph form on the culture of these plants;
perhaps for the general gardener it might prove
too detailed. Included are descriptions of the
processes of these plants (photosynthesis,
fenestration, reproduction processes, etc.). It
does have a more scientific approach than usual
and is not meant to help identify these diverse
plants.

373. Padilla, Victoria. THE COLORFUL BROMELIADS; THEIR
INFINITE VARIETY. Los Angeles: Bromeliad Society,
1981. 111p.
Good color photographs identify many of the more
commonly grown plants in the bromeliad family.
General history, native habitat, and brief
cultural information are also featured. A good
beginner's guide to these plants.

## FUCHSIAS

374. Jennings, K., and V. Miller. GROWING FUCHSIAS.
London: Croom Helm, 1979. 168p.
Fuchsias are grown mainly as outdoor shrubs and as
greenhouse plants in England, while in much of
North America they are often grown as outdoor
hanging basket plants during the summer. All
recent publications on fuchsia have been written
in England. This title is the best for general
cultural information. Details of propagation,
potting, fertilizing, and the control of pests
(important!) are included. There is less
information on the identification of cultivars
than the following titles.

375. Ewart, Ron. FUCHSIA LEXICON. New York:
Van Nostrand Reinhold, 1982. 336p.
After a short introductory section on fuchsia
culture, this title contains over 300 pages of
descriptions of many cultivars and species. 192
are illustrated in clear color photographs.

376.  Proudley, Brian, and Valerie Proudley. FUCHSIAS IN
      COLOR. New York: Hippocrene Books, 1975. 206p.
      199 small color photographs help identify fuchsia
      species and cultivars. The small book would be
      convenient to carry to shows.
377.  Saunders, Eileen. WAGTAILS BOOK OF FUCHSIAS.
      Henfield, England: E.R.M. Saunders, 1971-76. 4 vols.
      Specialized collections and serious collectors of
      fuchsias will appreciate these large handsome
      volumes. Large watercolors of leaf, flower, and
      bud characteristics help identify each fuchsia.
      The descriptive text also has line drawings to aid
      in identification. An outstanding series.

                        GERANIUMS
      (see the quarterly (570) of the International
      Geranium Society.)

378.  Wilson, Helen Van Pelt. THE JOY OF GERANIUMS: THE
      STANDARD GUIDE TO THE SELECTION, CULTURE AND USE
      OF THE PELARGONIUM. New York: Morrow Quill
      Paperbacks, 1980. 363p.
      Published in 1946, this book is still useful as it
      was written for American gardeners and
      concentrated on the types of geraniums that
      American gardeners grow. Good cultural
      information is featured with an informally treated
      classification of the genus PELARGONIUM. Many of
      the more popular pre-1965 cultivars are described.
      A good gardener's guide to the plants; specialists
      might look elsewhere for more detailed information.
379.  Shellard, Alan. GERANIUMS FOR HOME AND GARDEN.
      North Pomfret, VT: David & Charles, 1981. 232p.
      For geranium specialists this English guide will
      be of interest. It might cause difficulties
      for novice gardeners both in its use of English
      terminology and its descriptions of varieties
      seldom grown in North America. The title is
      excellent, however, on propagating, hybridizing,
      and instructing gardeners as to how to grow
      geraniums as standards.
380.  Clifford, Derek. PELARGONIUMS INCLUDING THE POPULAR
      'GERANIUM'. 2nd ed. London: Blandford Press,
      1970. 299p.
      This older title has detailed descriptions of many
      of the species and cultivars of PELARGONIUM.

Many of the English plants will be hard to obtain.
Specialists only.

381.   Wood, Henry James.   PELARGONIUMS: A COMPLETE GUIDE
TO THEIR CULTIVATION.   2nd ed.   Beaverton, OR:
ISBS, 1981?
An   English   title   which   would   be   useful   to
specialists.   Information   on   hybridizing   and
exhibiting these plants is included.   Some of the
varieties will be hard to find in North America.

IVY

382.   Pierot, Suzanne.   THE IVY BOOK: THE GROWING AND CARE
OF IVY AND IVY TOPIARY.   New York: Macmillan,
1974.   164p.
The   cultivation   of ivy indoors and   outdoors   is
presented in this small-sized monograph.   Written
by   a   former   President of   the   American   Ivy
Society, it is a practical and insightful title on
the culture and uses of ivy,   concentrating mainly
on   growing ivy indoors.   This title also defines
the many ivies by broad-leaf   characteristics.   A
chapter on ivy topiary and a list of suppliers are
included.

383.   Rose, Peter Q.   IVIES.   Poole:   Blandford Books,
1980.   180p.
This   English   title   is   for   the   dedicated   ivy
enthusiast.   The growing of ivies is different in
England,   so   readers will have to   translate to
their North American conditions. Brief information
is   given   on culture.   The descriptions   of   the
myriad   cultivars   of ivy will be useful for   those
seeking such information.   The Pierot title (382),
was written for American gardeners.

CACTI AND SUCCULENTS
(see   also   the bimonthly (565) of the   Cacti   and
Succulent Society of America.)

384.   Andersohn, Gunter.   CACTI AND SUCCULENTS.   New York:
Sterling Pub., 1983.   312p.
The   practicalities of cacti and succulent culture
are   well   covered in this   recent   title.   Basic
succulent   structure   and   growth   pattern   are
introduced.   Requirements   for   these   plants   are
excellently   covered   including   light,   soils,

temperature, watering, nutrients, containers, and more. Methods of propagation are also well covered. Two long encylopedic sections on both specific cacti and succulent genera identify and give native habitat and general care of most important and more commonly grown plants. Translated from the original German, this title makes an excellent introduction to the cultivation of these plants.

385. Martin, Margaret J.; P.R. Chapman; and H.A. Auger. CACTI AND THEIR CULTIVATION. New York: Scribner, 1971. 204p.

This older English title is one of the better guides to beginning cactus cultivation. Straightforward advice is given for cultivation requirements and propagation. Excellent discussions of the various types of cacti are included. Chapters include cacti of North America, South America, epiphytes, cristate cacti, and others. Effective black and white and color photographs illustrate some of these cacti and also such processes as grafting cacti. A good beginner's guide.

386. Martin, Margaret J., and Peter R. Chapman. SUCCULENTS AND THEIR CULTIVATION. New York: Scribner, 1977. 299p.

Companion volume to the author's CACTI AND THEIR CULTIVATION (385), this title concisely covers a widely diverse grouping of plants. Six major succulent families, Agavaceae, Aizoaceae, Asclepiadaceae, Crassulaceae, Euphorbiaceae, and Liliaceae are each described in separate chapters, with other succulents grouped together in another two chapters. A brief introductory chapter describes general growing methods and culture. Very brief cultural advice is given for the generic level. This title is one of the most concise guides, and it is idealy suited for quick reference.

387. Backeberg, Curt. CACTUS LEXICON. Poole: Blandford, 1976. 828p.

One of the most inclusive titles on cacti, this title is comprised of two sections, a descriptive listing arranged by genera and a photographic encyclopedia also arranged by genera. This title is useful mainly as an identification guide and to provide descriptive information on the many genera

and species covered. It is not a guide to
cultivation. There are 535 illustrations of
species and about 450 pages in the descriptive
encyclopedic section. There are also 18 world
distribution maps of various cacti subfamilies.
This English edition is a translation of the third
German edition.

388.   Jacobsen, Hermann. LEXICON OF SUCCULENT PLANTS:
       SHORT DESCRIPTIONS, HABITS AND SYNONYMY OF
       SUCCULENT PLANTS OTHER THAN CACTACEAE. London:
       Blandford, 1974. 664p.
       366 genera and 8,600 species are described in this
       thorough title    on succulents (Cactaceae are
       excluded). Information in each generic entry
       includes naming authority, family, native habitat,
       botanical description of many plant parts, and
       brief cultural requirements. Cultural information
       consists mainly of such brief statements as
       "requires a warm greenhouse." Propagation of
       these plants is also discussed. 1,200 small black
       and white photographs help in identification.
       Also included is a bibliography and a listing of
       some archaic names. Most of the information in
       this text is taken from this author's three volume
       translated work, A HANDBOOK OF SUCCULENT PLANTS.

389.   Rauh, Werner. THE WONDERFUL WORLD OF SUCCULENTS.
       2nd. rev. ed. Washington, DC: Smithsonian Press,
       1984. 164p.
       This is a translation of the second German edition
       (1979) of Dr. Rauh's popular book on succulents.
       After brief introductory chapters on the
       cultivation of succulents, their diseases and
       pests, and how these plants grow, the author lists
       the cultivated species of succulents by family.
       For each family primary genera and species are
       described. Also for many specific family
       discussions there are descriptions of morphology,
       cultivation, and pests and diseases. Many good
       black and white and color photographs help
       identify these plants.

390.   Rowley, Gordon. THE ILLUSTRATED ENCYCLOPEDIA OF
       SUCCULENTS. New York: Salamander, 1978. 256p.
       The more popular succulents are discussed by
       family in this    attractively illustrated title.
       Large color photographs with a popularly written
       text help identify these diverse plants. Good
       introductory chapters on succulent morphology,

ecology, genetics, and systematics keep the nonspecialist in mind. This English title's brief cultural advice is easy to translate to North American terms. Both a photographic encyclopedia and a good introduction to these plants.

391. Lamb, Edgar, and Brian M. Lamb. THE POCKET ENCYCLOPEDIA OF CACTI AND SUCCULENTS IN COLOR. New York: Macmillan, 1970. 217p.
Valuable mainly as a pictorial encyclopedia featuring over 300 small color photographs of some of the more popularly grown species. Brief cultural advice is given for each pictured species. General information on general culture, greenhouse culture, and propagation is also included. The authors maintain a famous collection of these plants in England. Their cultural advice can be easily understood by gardeners in North America.

392. Evans, Ronald L. HANDBOOK OF CULTIVATED SEDUMS. Northwood, Middlesex, England: Science Reviews, 1983. 345p.
For those specializing in sedum, this handbook would be very useful. Detailed descriptions (habit, stem, branches, leaves, flowers, inflorescence, buds, sepals, petals, stamens, anthers, carpels!), flowering times, and habitat are included. Also for each species specific care and effectiveness of the plants in cultivation are discussed. Introductory materials include a detailed illustrated glossary and information on the botany, ecology, habitat, and pests and diseases. Also found are excellent line drawings, color photographs and a bibliography.

393. Riha, J., and R. Subik. THE ILLUSTRATED ENCYCLOPEDIA OF CACTI & OTHER SUCCULENTS. London: Octopus Books, 1981. 352p.
Featuring a selected listing of cacti and succulents, this title would be a good beginner's guide. Generalized cultural information is given (watering, temperature, fertilizing, etc.). Among the 14 chapters comprising the descriptive listing of these plants are those on cacti of North and Central America, bromeliads, succulent orchids, and living pebbles. Each entry gives botanical name, naming authority for the species, description in nontechnical language, and limited specific cultural information. Excellently

illustrated with many black and white and also
color photographs. Translated from the Czech.
394.  Kramer, Jack. CACTI AND OTHER SUCCULENTS. New York:
Abrams, 1977. 159p.
A nontechnical cultivation guide and descriptive
work on many of the more commonly grown cacti and
succulents. Cultural information is included
for the beginner. The over 175 color and black
and white photographs are excellent. Appended is
a brief source list and bibliography. A good
beginner's guide.
395.  Venning, Frank Denmire. CACTI. New York: Golden
Press, 1974. 395p.
A truly pocket sized paperback that helps identify
over 200 of the more commonly grown species. Many
colored artist's representations help in this
process. The text describes these plants in a
nontechnical manner.
396.  Innes, Clive. THE COMPLETE HANDBOOK OF CACTI AND
SUCCULENTS: A COMPREHENSIVE GUIDE TO CACTI AND
SUCCULENTS IN THEIR HABITATS...New York: Van
Nostrand Reinhold, 1977. 224p.
This title would be useful for selecting and
identifying succulent plants. Over 180 pages are
devoted to describing succulents as divided into
epiphytes, North American, South American, and old
world native plants. Cultural information is too
brief and general to be of much use.
397.  Chidamian, Claude. THE BOOK OF CACTI AND OTHER
SUCCULENTS. Reprint ed. Beaverton, OR: Timber
Press, 1984.
An older title (1958) that still provides a good
basic beginning text on the cultivation of these
popular plants. The author lists those plants he
thinks the indoor gardener might find of interest
and gives basic cultural advice. He discusses
growing them indoors and to a lesser extent in the
garden. First published in 1958.
398.  Benson, Lyman David. THE CACTI OF THE UNITED STATES
AND CANADA. Stanford, CA: Stanford University
Press, 1982. 243p.
A technical monograph which might be of interest
to those specializing in cacti. It is primarily a
taxonomic guide with information on 18 genera and
152 species. It includes many line drawings and
photographs which aid in identification.

CARNIVOROUS PLANTS

399.    Swenson, Allan A.  CULTIVATING CARNIVOROUS PLANTS.
        Garden City, NY: Doubleday, 1977.  160p.
        This is a good popular introduction to these
        specialized plants for the novice.  Venus
        flytraps, sundews, pitcher plants, butterworts,
        and others are included.  Detailed growing
        information is provided.  For students, various
        experiments are suggested.  A nondescriptive
        listing of the world's carnivorous plants is
        included.  The best growing guide.
400.    Slack, Adrian.  CARNIVOROUS PLANTS.  Cambridge, MA:
        MIT Press, 1979.  240p.
        A handsomely illustrated title that serves as a
        good introduction to these plants.  The black and
        white and color photographs     capture the mystery
        and allure of these plants as well as help to
        identify them.  Cultivation information is
        inclusive enough for the novice.  A pleasing title
        that should interest readers in these plants.
401.    Schwartz, Randall.  CARNIVOROUS PLANTS.  New York:
        Praeger Pub., 1974.  128p.
        A more selected guide to growing carnivorous
        plants.  About 25 species are described with
        capsuled information given on native habitat,
        botanical description, brief cultivation, and
        propagation.  A brief treatment.
402.    Schnell, Donald E.  CARNIVOROUS PLANTS OF THE UNITED
        STATES AND CANADA.  Winston-Salem, NC: J.F. Blair,
        1976.  125p.
        Limited to U.S. and Canadian carnivorous plants,
        this title serves best as an identification
        manual.  Excellent color photographs with maps
        indicating native habitats are featured.  Species
        information is detailed and includes botanical and
        common names, habitat, description, and useful
        general information.  Cultural information
        appended is sufficient for beginners.
403.    Lloyd, Francis Ernest.  THE CARNIVOROUS PLANTS.
        New York: Dover Pub., 1976.  352p.
        First published in 1942, this classic title
        features detailed botanical information on the
        world's carnivorous plants.  This scientifically
        oriented text is useful for identification
        purposes and reference information about these
        plants, but it does not tell how to grow these

plants.

ORCHIDS
(see also the many excellent publications (654-56)
of The American Orchid Society, and the many
orchid periodicals (575-78) ).

404.  Northen, Rebecca Tyson.  HOME ORCHID GROWING.  3rd. ed.
      New York: Van Nostrand Reinhold, 1970.  374p.
      Long recognized as one of the most authoritative
      writers on orchids, this author's cultural guide
      has gone through three popular editions.  It
      contains good general orchid cultural information
      and also more specific growing information on the
      more popular orchid genera and hybrids.  Her
      selections of species would be helpful as a
      selection guide for beginners.  The discussion of
      the many orchid problems is excellent.  Not
      completely up to date but the best single guide to
      orchid culture.
405.  Fitch, Charles Marden.  ALL ABOUT ORCHIDS.  Garden
      City, NY:  Doubleday, 1981.  276p.
      One of the better guides to the culture of
      orchids.  Excellent, detailed information on
      proper lighting, containers, potting materials,
      watering and fertilizers, temperature and
      humidity, propagation, and orchid problems are
      included.  A brief encyclopedic section on orchid
      genera describes some of the more commonly grown
      orchids.  Detailed basic information on orchid
      culture makes this a good guide for the beginner
      and a good reference on growing orchids.
406.  Northen, Rebecca Tyson.  MINIATURE ORCHIDS.  New York:
      Van Nostrand Reinhold, 1980.  189p.
      Space conscious indoor gardeners concentrate on
      miniature plants, including orchids.  This
      excellent and detailed title gives good basic
      cultivation information with a long encyclopedic
      section describing these smaller orchids.
      Arranged alphabetically by genus, the encyclopedic
      sections include brief descriptions and also
      cultural information for each species.  Many small
      colored and black and white photographs help to
      identify discussed species.  Recommended highly.
407.  Bechtel, Helmut; Phillip Crib; and Edmund Launert.
      THE MANUAL OF CULTIVATED ORCHID SPECIES.
      Cambridge, MA: MIT Press, 1981.  444p.

Primarily a detailed listing of commonly
cultivated orchid genera and species, this
encyclopedic book is an excellent source of basic
information on these plants. Generic information
includes a listing of the tribe, subtribe, brief
descriptions of plant parts, distribution,
taxonomy, and general culture. Information on
species includes brief description, distribution,
history and synonyms. Discussions of orchid
biology, ecology, hybridization, and nomenclature
are also featured. There are good line drawings
and many color photographs. A great reference
source for orchids with brief information on
culture.

408.  Sheehan, Thomas John, and Marion Sheehan. ORCHID
      GENERA ILLUSTRATED. New York: Van Nostrand
      Reinhold, 1979. 207p.
      This classification and identification guide to
      orchids of the world focuses on more than 60
      orchid genera. For each genus, a botanical
      drawing is included along with text giving
      pronounciation, tribe, subtribe, identification
      characteristics, and brief cultural information.
      Brief discussions of orchid classification and
      biology are included. A classification guide is
      limited to a few of the more common orchid genera.

409.  Shuttleworth, Floyd S.; Herbert S. Zim; and Gordon W.
      Dillon. ORCHIDS. New York: Golden Press, 1970.
      160p.
      This small paperback is an excellent
      identification guide to the largest plant family
      in the world. This title is a favorite of orchid
      enthusiasts because of its small colored
      illustrations of 420 orchid varieties. Not a
      guide to orchid cultivation.

410.  Hawkes, Alex D. ENCYCLOPEDIA OF CULTIVATED ORCHIDS:
      AN ILLUSTRATED DESCRIPTIVE MANUAL OF THE MEMBERS
      OF THE ORCHIDACEAE CURRENTLY IN CULTIVATION.
      London: Faber, 1965. 602p.
      An older guide to the many cultivated orchids that
      is still used although there have been many
      nomenclature changes since it was published.
      Native habitat, general descriptions, and cultural
      information are given for generic listings, while
      native habitat, detailed descriptions, and
      synonyms are given for specific entries. Somewhat
      superseded by Bechtel et al.(407).

411.  Dressler, Robert L.  THE ORCHIDS: NATURAL HISTORY AND
      CLASSIFICATION.  Cambridge, MA: Harvard
      University Press, 1981.  332p.
      For those looking for a reference work with good
      intelligible discussions of orchid biology,
      ecology, and classification, this is an excellent
      choice.  Mainly a classification of Orchidaceae,
      it discusses them under broad subfamily
      classifications.  It contains keys to subfamilies,
      tribes, and subtribes.  A good bibliography on
      these orchid topics and also a listing of orchid
      floras are appended.

412.  Sander, David F., and Marjorie Wreford.  DAVID
      SANDER'S ONE-TABLE LIST OF ORCHID HYBRIDS,
      1946-1960.  Sussex, David Sander's Orchids, 1961.
      Supplements: 1961-63, 1964-66, etc.
      For orchid specialists, these reference works on
      orchid hybrids will be consulted often.  Arranged
      alphabetically by genera, they list registered
      hybrids of the period covered, giving parentage,
      orchid breeder, and date of introduction -- this
      inforation is for serious growers and breeders of
      orchids.  Supplements are published by The Royal
      Horticultural Society in London.


                              Ferns
      (see also the periodicals of the Los Angeles
      International Fern Society (568-69), and The
      American Fern Society (567).  Ferns as treated
      here also include fern cultivation out-of-doors).

413.  Hoshizaki, Barbara Joe.  FERN GROWERS MANUAL.
      New York: Knopf, 1975.  256p.
      Mrs. Hoshizaki's book on ferns is one of the
      finest gardening titles published in the United
      States.  Carefully written and researched, it
      includes most of the major fern genera and species
      throughout the world.  This title is both a
      growing guide and an identification manual.  Her
      growing advice for ferns in general covers soils,
      fertilizers, watering, humidity, and methods of
      growing ferns in the home, greenhouse, and out of
      doors.  Cultural advice in the generic listing is
      given by key words (semi-tender, drained potting
      mix, moist-dry, etc.).  Identification can be made
      both by consulting the carefully written
      descriptions and with the aid of many black and

white photographs showing growth habit and close-
ups of identifying features. The biology of
ferns, propagation (including sowing spores),
landscaping with ferns, and possible problems are
other topics discussed. Detailed, yet a pleasure
to read.
414. Foster, F. Gordon. FERNS TO KNOW AND GROW. 3d. ed.
rev. and enl. Portland, OR: Timber Press, 1984.
227p.
Mr. Foster is one of America's most respected
plantsmen, and his title on ferns and fern culture
for the gardener has been very popular with
gardeners. It has been updated and revised into a
much more attractive and comprehensive volume in
its latest edition. Detailed sections describe
hardy ferns to use in the landscape and tender
ferns for indoor culture. Identification is aided
by many anatomical drawings and silhouettes of
typical fern fronds. Besides the short cultural
advice given for specific ferns, there is also
good general advice on the growing of these plants
that sometimes give gardeners problems.
Propagation and the structure of ferns are also
covered. The first edition of this title was
titled THE GARDENER'S FERN BOOK.
415. Perl, Philip. FERNS. The Time-Life Encyclopedia of
Gardening. Alexandria, VA: Time-Life Books, 1977.
159p.
An alphabetic encyclopedic listing of ferns with
small watercolors of fern fronds for aid in
identification. Each fern is briefly described
with growing instructions. Introductory chapters
include photographic essays on how to use ferns in
the home and landscape. Basic, brief information.
416. Mickel, John, and Evelyn Fiore. THE HOME GARDENER'S
BOOK OF FERNS. New York: Holt, Rinehart & Winston,
1979. 256p.
This title does not try to identify as many ferns
as in the previous titles but concentrates on the
growing of ferns indoors and outdoors. Collecting
ferns from the wild and a listing of public
gardens where these plants can be seen throughout
the world are also included.

METHODS OF GROWING AND USING PLANTS

Bonsai
(see also bonsai periodicals (561-63))

417. Young, Dorothy S. BONSAI, THE ART AND TECHNIQUE.
     Englewood Cliffs, NJ: Prentice-Hall, 1985. 423P.
     The complex art of bonsai with its many different
     styles and growing techniques is defined in this
     well produced manual. The basics of bonsai
     culture are first covered including pruning,
     wiring, soil mixes, and containers. Then the care
     of bonsai and where bonsai can be kept are
     defined. The many complex bonsai styles are only
     introduced. A valuable section on woody plant
     species that are used in bonsai culture is an
     added feature. Here the plants are described with
     basic cultural information included. Appended are
     listings of societies, a glossary, a hardiness
     zone map, and more. A comprehensive and
     intelligent introduction to bonsai for the
     beginner and a good reference manual for more
     experienced growers of bonsai.
418. Naka, John Yoshio. BONSAI TECHNIQUES. Santa Monica:
     Published for the Bonsai Institute of California
     by Dennis-Landham, 1973. 262p.
419.   BONSAI TECHNIQUES II. Santa Monica: Published
     for the Bonsai Institute of California by
     Dennis-Landham, 1982. 442p.
     Written by a recognized American expert on bonsai,
     Mr. Naka's two volumes are for dedicated bonsai
     enthusiasts. Although the author covers the
     basics well, the thrust of these titles is to help
     the more knowledgeable growers of bonsai by giving
     instructions on how to train the plant material
     into the many traditional bonsai styles. The
     precise drawings and photographs help illustrate
     the author's points. The second volume ignores
     the basics and concentrates on more advanced
     techniques. There is enough detail to make these
     volumes valuable for dedicated bonsai growers for
     years of training bonsai. Writing about an
     advanced art such as bonsai is difficult, but
     these volumes are two of the best detailed guides
     to the diverse styles of bonsai.
420. Koreshoff, Deborah R. BONSAI, ITS ART, SCIENCE,
     HISTORY AND PHILOSOPHY. Portland, OR: Timber
     Press, 1984. 255p.
     Excellently designed and illustrated, this

handsome guide introduces the art of bonsai
through appreciation of its history and
philosophy. Schooled in the different Japanese
styles, the author illustrates their basic
production techniques. This title has very
handsome color photographs illustrating many
bonsai styles. Also the many drawings included
help define the described pruning and wiring
techniques. Although basic bonsai production is
introduced, this manual would be more useful to
advanced students of bonsai.

421.  THE ESSENTIALS OF BONSAI. By the editors of
      Shufunotomo. Portland, OR: Timber Press, 1982. 108p.
      This title provides a good introduction to the art
      of bonsai. Basics of bonsai raising, training,
      and care are all briefly covered along with some
      of the aesthetics and definitions of bonsai
      styles. Very well illustrated with photographs
      and drawings, this title makes a brief and to the
      point introduction to the subject.

422.  "Bonsai for Indoors." Edited by Constance T.
      Derederian. PLANTS & GARDENS 32, No. 3: 1-76.
      Autumn 1976.
      Many different bonsai experts contributed to this
      manual on indoor bonsai. The many tropical plants
      from which to select possible bonsai are described
      along with basic pruning, potting, wiring and
      introductory care. The aesthetics of different
      bonsai styles is briefly introduced. An excellent
      introduction to indoor bonsai.

423.  Derderian, Constance F. "Subtropical Bonsai for
      Indoor Gardening." ARNOLDIA 36:1-21. Jan/Feb 1976.
      21p.
      The author gives basics of raising, training, and
      care along with a listing of those subtropicals
      suitable for year-around indoor bonsai culture.
      Photographs of some of the plants discussed
      growing as bonsai specimens are included. 20
      pages of condensed information.

## Greenhouses

424.  Northen, Henry T., and Rebecca T.Northen. GREENHOUSE
      GARDENING. 2nd ed. New York: Ronald Press, 1973.
      353p.
      One of the better general texts on greenhouses and
      the plants that can be grown in them. No

nonsense, practical information is carefully
presented on construction and greenhouse
management. A lot of information is given on the
many types of plants grown under glass. This
section on plants is more up to date than the
section on construction and materials. Good
practical (if unexciting) photographs, charts, and
tables are included. Especially valuable as an
introduction to the subject.

425. Eaton, Jerome A. GARDENING UNDER GLASS; AN
ILLUSTRATED GUIDE TO THE GREENHOUSE. New York:
Macmillan, 1973. 306p.
Another beginning text for those considering
adding a greenhouse. Basic information to
consider on types of greenhouses, greenhouse
construction, and greenhouse management is
featured. Also included are brief entries on the
diverse plants that can be grown in greenhouses.
Photographs are used effectively. A beginning,
useful guide.

426. Walls, Ian Gascoigne. THE COMPLETE BOOK OF
GREENHOUSE GARDENING. New York: Quadrangle/New
York Times Books, 1975. 447p.
One of the most inclusive titles on greenhouses
and their plants, this English title will be of
interest to serious greenhouse growers. More
detailed information is given on important
greenhouse plants such as chrysanthemums, orchids,
roses, carnations, vegetables, fruits, and more.
North American gardeners will have to translate
this title to American conditions and materials.
Also briefly covered are such subjects as
hydroponics and lighting in greenhouses. One of
the most detailed book on greenhouse growing, this
title will be of special interest to experienced
growers.

427. THE SOLAR GREENHOUSE BOOK. Edited by James C.
McCullagh. Emmaus, PA: Rodale Press, 1978. 328p.
A practical title that includes all the
information one needs when considering this type
of greenhouse. Basics on climatic factors that
influence construction and detailed practical
construction methods and materials are covered.
Case studies of working solar structures in
climatically diverse parts of the country are
included. Also basic information on vegetable
crops that can be grown in these structures are

detailed. Appendices include sun charts and
assessments of commercial glazing materials. A
very practical handbook written by many experts in
their fields.

428.  Pierce, John H. GREEN HOUSE GROW HOW: A REFERENCE
BOOK. Seattle: Plants Alive Books, 1977. 241p.
Detailed building schematics, many charts and
tables, great practical illustrations, and a lot
of other basic information on greenhouse
construction and management are packed into this
practical title. Detailed information on
greenhouse structures, coverings, light and
lighting, heating (including briefly solar
heating), cooling and shading, and much more is
included. Care of plants, fertilization, soils,
growth regulation, diseases and pests, and
propagation techniques are also included. This is
not a guide to growing specific greenhouse plants,
but for those who want to construct their own
greenhouses, this is one book they should consult.

429.  Taylor, Kathryn S., and Edith W. Gregg. WINTER
FLOWERS IN GREENHOUSE AND SUN-HEATED PIT. Rev ed.
New York: Scribner, 1969. 281p.
This older classic first written in 1941 is
interesting to browse through even if one is not
interested in starting a cool greenhouse or sun
pit. Detailed instructions are given on how to
construct sun pits, lean-to cool greenhouses, and
associated structures. The second section of this
text discusses the woody, herbaceous, and tender
and hardy bulbs that can be grown in such
environments. While there are many English titles
that detail cool greenhouses and alpine houses,
this title gives an American perspective to this
subject.

430.  Abraham, George, and Katy Abraham. ORGANIC GARDENING
UNDER GLASS: FRUITS, VEGETABLES, AND ORNAMENTALS
IN THE GREENHOUSE. New York: Van Nostrand Reinhold,
1984. 308p.
A specialized, yet practical text on organic
gardening practices in the greenhouse. The basics
of greenhouse construction and management are
included here, but it is for the organic
perspective that this book will be consulted.
Soil considerations are defined and
recommendations are given. Greenhouse plants are
discussed with especially detailed sections on

vegetables, fruit and herbs.
431.  McDonald, Elvin.  THE FLOWERING GREENHOUSE DAY BY DAY.
Princeton, NJ: Van Nostrand, 1966.  158p.
Because routine maintenance and seasonal plantings
of greenhouse plants are so important,  this older
title  has  still  much  merit.   It  takes  the
greenhouse grower through the year month by month.
Also  a  detailed  listing of plants  for  various
conditions (cool, moderate, or warm) is included.

## Hydroponics

432.  Resh, Howard M.  HYDROPONIC FOOD PRODUCTION: A
DEFINITVIE GUIDE BOOK OF SOILLESS FOOD GROWING...
2nd ed.  Santa Barbara: Woodbridge Press, 1981.
After introducing a short history and defining the
benefits  of  hydroponics,  the  author  discusses
proper  plant nutrition with recommended  nutrient
solutions  and  possible  growing  mediums.   He
briefly defines the many soilless cultures (water,
gravel,  sand,  sawdust, and others) and gives the
relative  merits  of  each.   A  source  list,
bibliography, and index is appended.
433.  Bridwell, Raymond.  HYDROPONIC GARDENING; THE "MAGIC"
OF MODERN HYDROPONICS FOR THE GARDENER.  Loma
Linda, CA:  Woodbridge Press, 1974.  224p.
The  components  of  hydroponic  culture  (growing
mediums,  nutrient solutions, general environment,
etc.)  are  briefly defined in this  short  title.
Mr. Bridwell defines the methods of raising plants
from seeds to their flowering/fruiting.   The text
is  too  casually  written  and  organized.   Many
photographs but no index or source list.

## Decorating with Plants

434.  Wallach, Carla.  INTERIOR DECORATING WITH PLANTS.
New York: Macmillan, 1976.  239p.
The  new field of interior decorating with  plants
or  plantscaping  is  introduced  in  this  upbeat
title.   Many photographs show examples of the use
of  plants as decorative elements.   Also included
are  a  listing of plant materials  and  necessary
basic  care  of  plant  specimens.   A  popularly
focused title.
435.  Manaker, George H.  INTERIOR PLANTSCAPES;
INSTALLATION, MAINTENANCE AND MANAGEMENT.

Englewood Cliffs, NJ: Prentice-Hall, 1981. 283p.
This more detailed text serves as an introductory
manual for beginning classes in plantscaping.
Basics of requirements for light, temperature,
atmosphere, planters, and growing mediums are
covered and related to plant survival. Subjects
such as installation and maintenance contracts
probably will not interest most gardeners.

436. Allen, Oliver E. DECORATING WITH PLANTS. The
Time-Life Encyclopedia of Gardening. Alexandria,
VA: Time-Life Books, 1978. 160p.
A glossy title which might provide ideas for
gardeners on how to make better use of their
plants in their surroundings. Basic flower
arrangement, indoor gardens, patio plants and much
more are briefly covered. Plants are listed in an
encyclopedic section which features more
decorative specimens. This short title is best
used to generate ideas. Gardeners will want to
look elsewhere for more useful information.

## Flower Arrangement

437. THE COMPLETE GUIDE TO FLOWER & FOLIAGE ARRANGEMENT.
Edited by Iris Webb. Garden City, NY: Doubleday,
1979. 256p.
An introductory text to flower arrangement written
by experts on differing aspects of arrangement.
Well illustrated with color photographs and
drawings, it leads the novice through the basics.
Topics covered include aspects of design, color,
modern and abstract design, Ikebana, drying and
preserving flowers, and much more. A short
glossary is included.

438. Ascher, Amalie Adler. THE COMPLETE FLOWER ARRANGER.
New York: Simon & Schuster, 1974. 288p.
For the amateur this title serves well as a brief
introduction to the art of flower arrangement.
Design basics are defined and illustrated.
Different types of arrangements including
miniatures, Japanese, and the uses of many types
of arrangement materials (flowers, fruit, foliage,
wood, dried material) are covered. Well
illustrated and designed. This title lacks a
needed glossary.

439. Riester, Dorothy W. DESIGN FOR FLOWER ARRANGERS.
2nd ed. New York: Van Nostrand Reinhold, 1971. 192p.

Often used as a text in courses in beginning flower arrangement, this title is a favorite with arrangers. Mrs. Riester's title is a creative book emphasizing aspects of design as found in all art forms. It carefully defines aspects of design through text and carefully selected art reproductions. Not a comprehensive introduction to flower arrangement but a beginner's approach to design.

440.  Steere, William C., comp. FLOWER ARRANGEMENT: THE IKEBANA WAY. New York: Madison Square Press, 1972. 284p.
The multi-faceted art form of Japanese flower arrangement is introduced here. After a history of Ikebana, the Ikenobo, Ohara, and Sogetsu Schools of arrangement are defined. The many styles, fundamental forms, and methods of practice of these schools are introduced. There are many good texts on Ikebana, but this book serves as a good introduction. No index.

441.  Berrall, Julia S. A HISTORY OF FLOWER ARRANGEMENT. Rev ed. New York: Viking Press, 1968. 175p.
Flower arrangers are often interested in creating period arrangements approximating as closely as possible the arranging styles of many different cultural periods. This unique title is divided into three historical sections. The first section traces arrangement in the West from antiquity to the Victorian era (Europe and later America). The second section briefly discusses Chinese and Japanese Ikebana arrangement. The last section, entitled "Where East Meets West," is a short discussion of contemporary arrangement. The text emphasizes stylistic elements, proper containers, and plant material that can be used. Contemporary illustrations amplify the text. There is an newer edition not seen by the reviewer.

442.  Marcus, Margaret Fairbanks. PERIOD FLOWER ARRANGEMENT. New York: M. Barrows, 1952. 256p.
Written from an art history perspective, this valuable monograph has not been equalled. It traces the use of plant material used in the life of diverse cultures. The use of flowers, fruit, and foliage are followed. Arranged in a basic chronological treatment, it follows historically the earliest "floral arts of ancient Egypt" to contemporary uses. There are many good

illustrations and a glossary is appended.

## Terrariums

443. Elbert, Virginie, and George A. Elbert. FUN
     WITH TERRARIUM GARDENING. New York: Crown,
     1973. 144p.
     The basics of terrarium construction are well
     covered in this attractive title. Excellent
     photographs lead one through the choice of a
     container to selecting growing media, plants, and
     accessories. The excellent photographs show
     construction methods. Care of terrariums is also
     covered. Many different types of terrariums are
     illustrated.
444. Fitch, Charles Marden. THE COMPLETE BOOK OF
     TERRARIUMS. New York: Hawthorn Books, 1974. 150p.
     Basics of terrarium construction and care are
     covered in this bright book. Excellent advice is
     given on how to make terrariums into truly
     miniature gardens. Knowledgeable advice is given
     for the selection of plant material.
445. Kayatta, Ken, and Steven Schmidt. SUCCESSFUL
     TERRARIUMS: A STEP-BY-STEP GUIDE. Boston:
     Houghton Mifflin, 1975. 212p.
     This glossy book again covers the basics of
     terrarium construction very well. Photographs
     show examples of terrariums and construction
     methods. Also brief chapters on vivariums
     (terrariums with animals), terrariums for
     youngsters, and plans for a terrarium planting
     party are included.

## Dish Gardens

446. McDonald, Elvin. LITTLE PLANTS FOR SMALL SPACES: HOW
     TO SELECT AND GROW MINI PLANTS AND TREES INDOORS
     AND OUT. Rev. ed. New York: M. Evans, 1975. 192p.
     Emphasizing the many types of plants suitable for
     small scaled indoor cultivation, this title is
     unique and very well written. Plants included
     range from gesneriads, orchids, begonias, bulbs,
     evergreens, roses and many more. Less information
     is given on how to use these plants and
     construction methods for miniature gardens.
     Excellent cultural information, propagation
     advice, and photographs are included. The title's

1974 publication date means that many newer hybrids have been developed, and consequently, some of the plants described in this text might be hard to obtain. Substitutions of newer hybrids will be necessary.

447. Howarth, Sheila. MINIATURE GARDENS. New York: Arco, 1977. 105p.

Unlike Elvin McDonald's title (446), the emphasis here is on the use of small plants in different types of containers. Hanging baskets, bonsai, terrariums, and dish gardens are some of the recommended types of indoor and outdoor growing methods and containers. Less information is included on specific plants. The many colorful photographs make this book useful to generate new methods of growing plants. An English publication.

448. Perl, Philip. MINIATURES AND BONSAI. The Time-Life Encyclopedia of Gardening. Alexandria, VA: Time-Life Books, 1979. 160p.

Covering a very large range of gardening subjects, this text is a brief overview to miniatures in general. Bonsai, miniature roses, dish gardens, terrariums, gardens under lights and outdoor vegetable and ornamental gardens are all included. Also featured is an encyclopedic section of plants suitable for these growing methods. As the above listing might suggest, the wide-ranging subject matter means that a lot of information is given much too briefly. The materials covered in this book are treated much better elsewhere.

## Indoor Light Gardening

449. Elbert, George A. THE INDOOR LIGHT GARDENING BOOK. New York: Crown, 1973. 250p.

One of the better indoor gardening books and the best one for information on growing plants under lights. Detailed information is given on light garden construction and the cultural requirements for plants grown under lights. The author clearly explains why plants need light and how to use artificial lights. Recommended plants for this type of culture are described in depth. Some of the newer (post-1973) types of lights used for growing plants indoors are not discussed a fact which should provide the impetus for a new

edition.
450. Fitch, Charles Marden. THE COMPLETE BOOK OF
     HOUSEPLANTS UNDER LIGHTS. New York: Hawthorn
     Books, 1975. 275p.
     Another good text on light gardening but less
     detailed in regard to actual light garden
     construction than the Elbert title (449). His
     description of the plants he recommends for light
     gardens is very good. Those interested in this
     indoor method of growing plants will want to
     consult both this text and Mr. Elbert's.
451. Murphy, Wendy B. GARDENING UNDER LIGHTS. The
     Time-Life Encyclopedia of Gardening. Alexandria,
     VA: Time-Life Books, 1978. 160p.
     This glossy title is broadly divided into an
     encyclopedic section of plants suitable for light
     gardens and a general discussion of the
     construction of these gardens. Beautiful
     photographs give good ideas for light gardens, but
     construction methods are too briefly covered. The
     previously mentioned titles give better coverage
     to this subject, but beginners might find ideas
     here.

                        Dried Materials

452. Wiita, Betty. DRIED FLOWERS FOR ALL SEASONS.
     New York: Van Nostrand Reinhold, 1982. 138p.
     The techniques of preparing dried plant materials
     including using air drying, silica gel, glycerin,
     microwave ovens, and pressing flowers are
     carefully explained in this attractive title.
     Many decorative projects using these dried
     materials are shown in detail. There is less
     discussion of which materials can be dried and how
     to dry them than in other texts. Appended are
     supply sources and a quick reference chart which
     lists plant material with time and method of
     drying procedures. This is one of the most
     attractive manuals on drying plants altough other
     texts might want to be consulted for more detail
     on plant material.
453. Floyd, Harriet. PLANT IT NOW, DRY IT LATER.
     New York: McGraw-Hill, 1973. 231p.
     Informally written, this is a good guide to
     techniques of drying plant material, explaining
     which techniques can be used for specific plants,

how to store, and finally use this dried material.
The author discusses plant material by the order
of seasonal appearance which helps alert the dryer
as to what to look for next.   A few arrangements
are detailed with suggested construction methods
and choice of plant material.

454.  Condon, Geneal.  THE COMPLETE BOOK OF FLOWER
      PRESERVATION.  Boulder, CO: Pruett, 1982.
      This older book was somewhat updated and is still
      useful for its detailed description of how to
      preserve a diverse assortment of plant material.
      Written from practical experience, the author
      details which drying technique she has used for
      specific plants.  Mrs. Condon advises using sand
      for many drying projects.  Newer (and easier)
      techniques are described in other texts.

455.  Embertson, Jane.  PODS: WILDFLOWERS AND WEEDS IN
      THEIR FINAL BEAUTY. New York: Scribner, 1979.  186p.
      Color photographs of both the flowers and the
      naturally dried    pods, branches, and leaves help
      the arranger to identify and select naturally
      dried plant materials.   More than 150 commonly
      found species of the Northeastern United States
      are included with photographs and such information
      as  blooming  dates,  flower,  leaf  and  pod
      descriptions, where pods are usually found and how
      they can be used in arrangements.   Within its
      limited scope, this is an excellent guide.   The
      photographs are small.

456.  Mierhof, Annette.  THE DRIED FLOWER BOOK: GROWING,
      PICKING, DRYING, ARRANGING.  New York: Dutton,
      1981.  96p.
      Tastefully illustrated with watercolors of the
      plant material and the finished dried
      arrangements, this title briefly covers which
      plants can be used as dried materials and the
      techniques used for drying them.  Translated from
      the Dutch, the plant material is divided into
      annuals, perennials, herbs, wild flowers, grasses
      and seeds and more.  Information is brief and
      oriented toward European gardeners, so other works
      on these topics should be consulted.

GARDEN PRACTICES AND PLANT PROBLEMS

Tree Maintenance

457. Harris, Richard Wilson. ARBORICULTURE: CARE OF
TREES, SHRUBS AND VINES IN THE LANDSCAPE.
Englewood Cliffs, NJ: Prentice-Hall, 1983. 688p.
Although this textbook is written for use at the
college level, the serious gardener will find a
lot of practical information on the care of trees.
The preparation of the planting site and the
selection of the proper tree for the site are
emphasized. Fertilizing, watering, pruning, and
problems of trees are covered in detail. A good
reference on tree care, more up to date than Dr.
Pirone's title (458).

458. Pirone, Pascal Pompey. TREE MAINTENANCE. 5th ed.
New York: Oxford University Press, 1978. 587p.
Pests, diseases, chemical and environmental damage
along with other problems of trees are treated in
depth in this text. Dr. Pirone is a recognized
expert on diseases and pests and the care and
maintenance of American ornamental plants.
Different maintenance processes such as pruning,
bracing and cableing, cavity treatments,
fertilizing, and transplanting are discussed. A
valuable chapter lists trees for specific
locations such as trees that are low growing, for
wet areas, windbreaks, seashore planting, city
streets, etc.

Pruning

459. Allen, Oliver E. PRUNING AND GRAFTING. The
Time-Life Encyclopedia of Gardening. Alexandria,
VA: Time-Life, 1978. 160p.
In this title small drawings illustrate the first,
second, and third stage pruning of trees and large
shrubs. Also illustrated are cutting back
techniques, rejuvenations, shearings, and
pinchings of woody plant material. The many
drawings of the pruning techniques for a wide
ranging variety of plant material are very useful
to novice gardeners because each shows exactly
where and how much of the plant should be removed.
The pruning of plants into espalier and topiary is
shown in glossy photographs in the first section

of this title.
460.    Steffek, Edwin Francis.  THE PRUNING MANUAL.
        2d. rev. ed.  New York: Van Nostrand Reinhold,
        1982.  152p.
        A small paperback that is a great value in terms
        of both content and cost.  It briefly covers
        pruning instructions for most of the common
        landscape trees, shrubs, evergreens, vines, roses,
        grapes, and fruits.  Since this title was designed
        as a brief reference guide, one should look
        elsewhere for more detailed information.
461.    Brown, George E.  THE PRUNING OF TREES, SHRUBS AND
        CONIFERS.  New York: Winchester Press, 1972.  351p.
        This title is a thorough treatise on pruning.
        Written by a former assistant curator at the
        Royal Botanic Gardens, Kew, its text shows much
        practical knowledge and experience.  For example,
        the discussion of HYDRANGEA covers in detail
        different pruning practices for many of the
        species and hybrids of this genus.  Most
        information is correct; however, most American
        arborists would disagree with the recommended care
        after the major pruning of trees.  This is one of
        the most detailed of pruning manuals giving useful
        information on the pruning techniques for a wide
        ranging selection of plants.
462.    Grounds, Roger.  THE COMPLETE HANDBOOK OF PRUNING.
        New York: Macmillan, 1975.  157p.
        With its excellent illustrations, this guide
        serves as a good introduction to the basics of
        pruning for novice gardeners.  Although this title
        is of English origin, it is valuable to North
        American gardeners as most common landscape plants
        are covered.  Unusual topics are topiary in a
        brief chapter and also pruning of greenhouse
        plants.
463.    Baumgardt, John Philip.  HOW TO PRUNE ALMOST
        EVERYTHING.  New York: M. Barrows, 1968.  192p.
        An older title that still is useful for home
        gardeners, with the pruning of most landscape
        plants included.  Well illustrated.
464.    Hadfield, Miles.  TOPIARY AND ORNAMENTAL HEDGES:
        THEIR HISTORY AND CULTIVATION.  New York:
        St. Martin's Press, 1971.  100p.
        The specialized art of topiary is introduced in
        this English title.  Basic practical cultural
        advice for both topiary and ornamental hedging is

included. Some of the plant material featured
will not be suitable for most North American
climatic conditions. There are more illustrations
of ornamental hedges than of topiary. The
specialized topiary of ivy can be found in
Pierot's title on ivy (382).

## Plant Propagation

465. Toogood, Alan R. PROPAGATION. New York: Stein and
      Day, 1981. 320p.
      Plant propagation methods for amateurs are clearly
      defined in this English title. Both seed
      propagation and vegetative propagation
      (cuttings, budding, etc.) are covered. General
      propagation instructions are clearly given and
      good illustrations are included. Specific
      information in concise tabular form is given for
      "1500" hardy and nonhardy plants. This is a
      beginning text so those looking for in depth
      information of a more technical nature should look
      elsewhere.

466. Foster, Catharine Osgood. PLANTS-A-PLENTY: HOW TO
      MULTIPLY OUTDOOR AND INDOOR PLANTS THROUGH
      CUTTINGS, CROWN AND ROOT DIVISIONS, GRAFTING,
      LAYERING, AND SEEDS. Emmaus, PA: Rodale Press,
      1977. 328p.
      PLANTS-A-PLENTY is a popularly focused title
      covering basic techniques of plant propagation
      along with the proper methods for propagating
      commonly grown plants. Propagation techniques are
      clearly defined with help from the many black and
      white photographs included in the text. Brief but
      accurate information is included for propagating
      specific fruits, nuts, ornamental woody plants,
      garden flowers, wild flowers, ferns, vegetables,
      herbs, and indoor plants. A detailed index guides
      one to specific plant entries. Nontechnical
      information is presented here in an accurate and
      understandable manner.

467. United States Forest Service. SEEDS OF WOODY PLANTS
      IN THE UNITED STATES. Washington: Forest Service,
      U.S. Dept. of Agriculture, 1974. Agr. Handbook No.
      450. 883p.
      Seed propagation is detailed for 188 genera of
      woody plants that are grown commercially in the
      United States. For each genus, information on

growth habit, use, races and hybrids, flowering
and fruiting characteristics, proper collection of
fruit, extraction and storage of seed, special
seed treatments, nursery practices, and much more
is given. Also general discussions of seed
biology, genetics, and testing are included. A
technical work for those looking for very specific
information.

468. Hartmann, Hudson Thomas, and Dale E. Kester. PLANT
PROPAGATION: THE PRINCIPLES AND PRACTICES. 4th ed.
Englewood Cliffs, NJ: Prentice-Hall, 1975.
This is one of the standard college-level
textbooks on plant propagation which may be useful
for amateurs looking for more detailed
information. Technical information on propagation
methods, media, containers, seed handling,
cuttings, grafting, budding, along with a short
discussion of micro-propagation is included.
Specific propagation techniques for commonly grown
fruits, nuts, woody plants, annuals, and
perennials are given. Certainly a good text on
propagation, but it might prove too technical for
the amateur.

469. McDonald, Elvin. HOW TO GROW HOUSE PLANTS FROM SEED.
New York: Mason/Charter, 1976.

470.                    HOW TO GROW FLOWERS FROM SEED.
New York: Van Nostrand Reinhold, 1979.

471.                    HOW TO GROW VEGETABLES AND HERBS
FROM SEED. New York: Mason/Charter, 1977.
All three of these books are similar in their
depth of coverage. Generally, each title contains
good explanations of propagation techniques for
specific plants in more depth than in many other
propagation guides. These books are useful to the
amateur as they present basic information in a
nontechnical manner.

472. Haring, Elda. THE COMPLETE BOOK OF GROWING PLANTS
FROM SEED. New York: Hawthorn Books, 1969. 240p.
As a popularly focused text, this book includes
most plants that the average gardener grows from
seed. The general discussion of seed sowing
practices is adequate but not given in depth, as
for instance the technique of seed stratification
is not listed in the index. Black and white
photographs.

## Soils

(see also organic gardening titles which generally
have good sections included on soils.)

473.  Ortloff, Henry Stuart, and Henry B. Raymore. A BOOK
      ABOUT SOILS FOR THE HOME GARDENER. New York:
      M. Barrows, 1962. 189p.
      An older title, but one of the best texts to
      explain soil structure and management to amateurs.
      Soil types are defined with chemical components
      listed. Fertilizers (inorganic and organic), soil
      acidity, drainage, and soil improvement methods
      are included. Unlike most titles on soils, the
      material is presented in a nontechnical manner
      understandable to the amateur.

474.  Logsdon, Gene. THE GARDENER'S GUIDE TO BETTER SOIL.
      Emmaus, PA: Rodale Press, 1975. 246p.
      The organic method of improving soil is defined in
      this nontechnical title. The organic gardening
      processes of mulching, composting, and using
      natural fertilizers and green manures are
      included. Information of a more technical nature
      and also information on inorganic materials should
      be found in other titles.

### Plant Diseases and Pests

475.  Pirone, Pascal Pompey. DISEASES AND PESTS OF
      ORNAMENTAL PLANTS. 5th ed. New York: Wiley,
      1978. 566p.
      Dr. Pirone's book, in its fifth edition, is still
      the best general title on diseases and pests of
      garden plants. While it does not include every
      problem that gardeners may encounter, it does
      concentrate on the more common problems. As a
      selective guide with many fewer listed problems
      for each plant it is easier for gardeners to find
      which problem is affecting their plants. Control
      measures are recommended (for the latest control
      measures, local extension type publications should
      be consulted). Pests and diseases of 500 indoor
      and outdoor gardening plants are included.

476.  Westcott, Cynthia. WESTCOTT'S PLANT DISEASE HANDBOOK.
      4th. ed. Edited by Ralph Kenneth Horst. New York:
      Van Nostrand Reinhold, 1979. 803p.
      Up to date and inclusive, this reference details
      plant diseases, the susceptibility of particular

plants to each disease, and common garden
chemicals (as of 1979) and their application. It
lists many diseases, not just the most common ones
that Pirone (475) does. It could be confusing to
the amateur to try to choose between so many
disease alternatives. This book should be
consulted when diseases are not found in less
inclusive, but easier to use, texts.

477. Westcott, Cynthia. THE GARDENER'S BUG BOOK. 4th ed.
Garden City, NY: Doubleday, 1973.
Although more outdated than Ms. Westcott's disease
handbook (476), this detailed title is still a
valuable listing of the many insects that can be a
problem to garden plants. It is divided into two
large sections, excellent disussions of the
biology of insects defined by broad groupings
(wasps, scale insects, etc), and a listing of
garden plants with their many problem insects.
Many of the common insects are pictured in
drawings. Recommended control methods should be
ignored in favor of more up-to-date sources.

478. THE ORTHO PROBLEM SOLVER. Edited by Michael D. Smith.
2nd ed. San Francisco: Ortho Informational
Services, 1984.
This large-format book presents color photographs
of plant problems in the garden. The arrangement
is by broad plant type (houseplants, ground
covers, weeds). For each diagnosed problem, a
color photograph illustrates the symptoms, the
problem is described, analyzed, and then given
control measures. Indication is given as to where
in the continental United States the problem is
found. Information is given succinctly and in
nontechnical language. Control measures,
unfortunately, are only Ortho brand products. The
book is prohibitively expensive ($150 +) for most
individuals or libraries. The compiler has seen
only the first 1982 edition.

479. Logsdon, Gene. GENE LOGSDON'S WILDLIFE IN YOUR GARDEN.
Emmaus, PA: Rodale Press, 1983. 268p.
The subtitle, "or dealing with deer, rabbits,
raccoons, moles, crows, sparrows, and other of
nature's creatures in ways that keep them around
but away from your fruits and vegetables" defines
the approach of this title. Commonsense
recommendations are given with no guarantees.

Fences and barriers are stressed. Ways to attract
desired animals, bees, birds and butterflies into
the landscape are discussed.

480. Ware, George Whitaker. COMPLETE GUIDE TO PEST CONTROL.
Fresno, CA: Thomson Pub., 1980. 290p.
This popular    text would be of help to solve the
more common pest problems. The more common pests
-- insects, diseases, algae, nematodes, weeds,
animals, and birds -- are defined and control
measures are recommended. Both chemical and nonchemical control measures are included. The index
accesses plants, their problems, and also
individual pests. Trying to cover too many topics
causes the text to lack detail in many areas.
Many common problems are treated well, while
others are not. For instance, both woodchucks and
prairie dogs are pictured but no controls for them
are given.

481. Forsberg, Junius L. DISEASES OF ORNAMENTAL PLANTS.
Rev. ed. Urbana: University of Illinois at
Urbana-Champaign, College of Agriculture, 1979.
Over 50 common garden plants, chiefly annuals and
perennials, are included in this disease handbook.
Disease problems caused by fungi, bacteria,
viruses, and nematodes are included by the author.
Numerous black and white photographs help in the
identification of these diseases. Because this
handbook is relatively out-of-date, more current
publications should be consulted for recommended
control measures.

482. Carr, Anna. RODALE'S COLOR HANDBOOK OF GARDEN
INSECTS. Emmaus, PA: Rodale Press, 1979. 241p.
Limited to insects that are found on vegetables,
nuts, and fruits, this title features color
photographs of many of the stages of these
insects, from eggs to adults. For each insect
range, description, life cycle, host plants,
feeding habits and natural controls are listed.
The control measures advocated are "natural"
controls. A brief identification key listing
common fruits and vegetables and their related
insects is also included. Ornamental plants with
their pests are not covered.

483. Pyenson, Louis. PLANT HEALTH HANDBOOK: A GUIDE TO
BETTER GARDENING INDOORS AND OUTDOORS. Westport,
CT: AVI Pub., 1981. 241p.
A manual designed to help keep plants healthy both

by correct cultural practices and by the control
of pests and diseases. Some of the cultural
practices defined include sanitation, biological
control of insects, and protection from
temperature and weather extremes. Pest control
while oriented to chemical controls also mentions
some nonchemical controls. A good general guide
for the gardener on pest control.

484. Johnson, Warren T., and Harold H. Lyon. INSECTS THAT
FEED ON TREES AND SHRUBS: AN ILLUSTRATED GUIDE.
Ithaca, NY: Comstock Pub. Associates, 1976. 464p.
This elaborately produced title contains good
color photographs of common insects and their
damage to ornamental trees and shrubs. 650
insects are included. Showing typical insect
damage, the book also lists geographical
distribution and the biology of these insects.
While control information is not provided, sources
of this information are given. The insects are
divided into those that damage conifers and those
found on broadleaf evergreen and deciduous plants.
This book provides good identification of insects,
with each insect pictured in many stages.

485. Dahl, Mogens H., and Thyge B. Thygesen. GARDEN PESTS
AND DISEASES OF FLOWERS AND SHRUBS. Edited by
A.M. Toms. New York: Macmillan, 1974. 223p.
Beautifully illustrated, this identification guide
makes these problems seem almost attractive.
Although this guide was produced in Europe, most
of the problems shown are also found in North
American gardens. Control measures are given very
short treatment. Useful for its colored drawings
of plant problems and pests.

486. Hamm, James G. THE HANDBOOK OF PEST CONTROL. New
York: F. Fell Pub., 1982. 272p.
A reference book designed to provide practical
information on the control of insects and pests.
Included are not only insects on plants but also
cockroaches, moths, and even some birds. Although
descriptions of the pests are given, they are not
pictured. There are dilution tables for mixing
pesticides appended. There is no index.

Weeds
(Control of weeds is best found in local county
extension type publications.)

487. Muenscher, Walter Conrad Leopold. WEEDS. 2d ed.
     Ithaca, NY: Comstock Pub. Associates, 1980. 586p.
     For detailed descriptions of weeds of North
     American this manual first published in 1935
     should be consulted. It contains more information
     on weeds than might interest the average gardener,
     but it is an excellent reference. There are line
     drawings of 331 varieties of weeds with
     descriptions of 571. Eradication by hand is the
     control measure usually recommended.
  *  THE ORTHO PROBLEM SOLVER. Cited above as item 478.
     Weed control using Ortho brand products is covered
     in this large reference.
488. Crockett, Lawrence J. WILDLY SUCCESSFUL PLANTS: A
     HANDBOOK OF NORTH AMERICAN WEEDS. New York:
     Macmillan, 1977. 268p.
     This popularly written title focuses on more than
     100 common weeds of North America. Weeds are
     identified by line drawings. The author included
     range and habitat, many suggested uses (such as
     food) and some control measures. A limited
     identification and reference guide for the novice
     gardener.
489. Martin, Alexander Campbell. WEEDS. New York: Golden
     Press, 1972. 160p.
     A small paperback suitable for carrying in pocket
     or purse for the identification of common weeds.
     The leaf, flower, fruit and seed characteristics
     are shown in color drawings along with information
     on the weed's distribution in the continental
     United States. The reasons why each plant is
     considered a weed are included.
490. GROWERS WEED IDENTIFICATION HANDBOOK. Berkeley:
     University of California, Division of Agricultural
     Sciences, 1983. Publication 4030.
     Many of the weeds of California are pictured in
     this looseleaf notebook. Clear color photographs
     illustrate each weed's identification characteris-
     tics. The text describes these plants and gives
     locations in California where they are most
     commonly found. This text is good for
     identification purposes but offers no weed control
     measures.

491.  NEBRASKA WEEDS. Rev. ed. Lincoln: Nebraska Dept. of
      Agriculture, Bureau of Plant Industry, 1979. 312p.
      This identification guide focuses on the weeds of
      the Midwestern United States.   Color photographs
      of variable quality are used  for identification
      purposes.   There  are also line drawings and some
      seeds pictured.   Each weed's distribution  and
      habitat  in  Nebraska  are  given.  There  is  an
      excellent illustrated glossary.

492.  Page, Nancy M., and Richard E. Weaver, Jr.  WILD
      PLANTS IN THE CITY. New York: Quadrangle/New York
      Times Books, 1975.  117p.
      An interesting title which focuses on those plants
      one finds growing wild in the urban environment of
      the   Northeastern   United   States.   Annuals,
      perennials,  grasses, trees, shrubs, and ferns are
      included.   Black and white photographs show these
      plants in their environments. There are also line
      drawings. Of more limited interest.


MISCELLANEOUS GARDENING TOPICS

Horticultural Therapy

493.  HORTICULTURAL THERAPY FOR NURSING HOMES, SENIOR
      CENTERS, RETIREMENT LIVING. By the Horticultural
      Therapy Department Staff of the Chicago
      Horticultural Society; Eugene A. Rothert, Jr.,
      and James R. Daubert.  Glencoe, IL: Chicago
      Horticultural Society, 1981.

494.  HORTICULTURAL THERAPY AT A PHYSICAL REHABILITATION
      FACILITY. By the Horticultural Therapy Department
      Staff of the Chicago Horticultural Society;
      Eugene A. Rothert, Jr., and James R. Daubert.
      Glencoe, IL: Chicago Horticultural Society, 1981.

495.  HORTICULTURAL THERAPY AT A PSYCHIATRIC HOSPITAL. By
      the Horticultural Therapy Department Staff of the
      Chicago Horticultural Society; James R. Daubert,
      and Eugene A. Rothert, Jr.  Glencoe, IL: Chicago
      Horticultural Society, 1981.

496.  HORTICULTURAL THERAPY FOR THE MENTALLY HANDICAPPED.
      By the Horticultural Therapy Department Staff of
      the Chicago Horticultural Society; James R.
      Daubert, and Eugene A. Rothert, Jr. Glencoe, IL:
      Chicago Horticultural Society, 1981.
      After introductory chapters and a defined case
      study on the specific horticultural therapy client

group, the authors provide basic indoor and outdoor gardening programs and craft projects that are repeated in each title. The core or repeated material is practically oriented and provides a good introduction to horticultural therapy. The original information in each handbook carefully defines what strategies should be used with the more specific client groups.

497. Cloet, Audrey, and Chris Underhill. GARDENING IS FOR EVERYONE: A WEEK-BY-WEEK GUIDE FOR PEOPLE WITH HANDICAPS. London: Souvenir Press, 1982. 208p. After introductory basic chapters, the authors take a therapy group through an entire year of week-by-week listings of activities and learning projects. The projects are practical and lead the therapy group through the growing year. American therapists will find many practical projects they can adapt for their own needs in this positive title.

498. Olszowy, Damon R. HORTICULTURE FOR THE DISABLED AND DISADVANTAGED. Springfield, IL: Thomas, 1978. 228p. Horticultural therapy is defined along with beginning information on horticulture techniques and training necessary for therapists. Client populations are briefly defined. A section on activities focuses on variously scaled projects suitable for different therapy groups. This title is oriented toward the beginning professional rather than a novice seeking elementary information on horticultural therapy.

Gardening with Children

499. Ocone, Lynn. THE YOUTH GARDENING BOOK: A COMPLETE GUIDE FOR TEACHERS, PARENTS AND YOUTH LEADERS. Burlington, VT: Gardens for All, 1983. 145p. Mainly concerned with beginning outdoor vegetable and flower garden projects, this instructional manual discusses how to establish the gardens and the programs built around these gardens. Practicalities of site and soil preparation are covered. Twenty eight garden experiments and tests are included. A resource list and index are appended.

500. Skelsey, Alice, and Gloria Huckaby. GROWING UP GREEN; CHILDREN & PARENTS GARDENING TOGETHER. New York: Workman Pub., 1973. 240p.

An informal manual for parents and children to discover "green things," the world of gardening and of nature in general. Simple projects, short profiles of personalities in the plant world, and much more are included.

## Tools for Gardeners

501. Crockett, James Underwood. CROCKETT'S TOOL SHED.
Boston: Little, Brown, 1979. 247p.
Specific tools for a wide ranging variety of applications are defined in this practical title. Manufacturer, price, model number, description, and use are included for each type of tool. Mr. Crockett's comments on these tools and their uses has the most long lasting value although the specifics will soon be out of date. Manufacturer's addresses are appended.
502. TOOLS & TECHNIQUES FOR EASIER GARDENING. Edited by Lynn Ocone and George Thabault. Burlington, VT: Gardens for All, 1984. 45p.
Less extensive than the preceding title (501), this title also lists recommended makes of tools for gardeners. Tools for horticultural therapy projects are briefly covered.

## Garden and Plant Photography

503. Fitch, Charles Marden. THE RODALE BOOK OF GARDEN PHOTOGRAPHY. New York: AMPHOTO, 1981. 160p.
Specifics on camera equipment and photographic techniques are discussed by this well known plant photographer. Of course, this title is illustrated with many photographs. A short bibliography is appended.
504. Fell, Derek. HOW TO PHOTOGRAPH FLOWERS, PLANTS & LANDSCAPES. Tucson, AZ: H.P. Books, 1980. 160p.
More specifics on photographing different plant material and landscape are included in this informal title. There is less discussion of equipment and techniques than Mr. Fitch's title (503). More numerous color photographs are also included.

## Attracting Birds to the Landscape

505. Degraaf, Richard M., and Gretchin M. Witman. TREES,

SHRUBS, AND VINES FOR ATTRACTING BIRDS: A MANUAL
FOR THE NORTHEAST. Amherst: University of
Massachusetts Press, 1979. 194p.
The many plants that can be used to feed, protect,
and generally attract birds to home landscapes are
defined in this carefully produced title. Trees,
shrubs and vines are discussed in separate
chapters. This title is beautifully written and
designed. Biased toward Northeastern U.S.
landscapes.

## Shakespearean Plants and Gardens

506. Chamberlain, Lucy, and Stephen K-M Tim. WILLIAM
SHAKESPEARE: THROUGH HIS GARDENS AND PLANTS.
Brooklyn: Brooklyn Botanic Garden, 1981.
While there are many older titles on these plants
and gardens, this small, well written and designed
folder provides a succinct and charming
introduction. Many period illustrations are used
along with Shakespearean quotes. A short plant
index is appended.

## Bible Plants for Gardens

507. Swenson, Allan A. YOUR BIBLICAL GARDEN: PLANTS OF
THE BIBLE AND HOW TO GROW THEM. Garden City, NY:
Doubleday, 1981. 217p.
While not very practical for most climatic regions
of North America, biblical gardens and plants are
of perennial interest to some gardeners. This
title does as well as any to try to define the
plants mentioned in the Bible and then how to grow
them. For serious study of the subject there are
many more botanically oriented texts.

## Food Preservation

508. STOCKING UP: HOW TO PRESERVE THE FOODS YOU GROW,
NATURALLY. New rev. and exp. ed. Emmaus, PA:
Rodale Press, 1977.
Storing, freezing, canning, and drying of home
vegetables and fruit produce are included in this

thorough  book.  Preserving   methods   are
described  carefully with recommendations of which
method  is  most successful for  each  variety  of
fruit  and  vegetable.  Also briefly covered  are
such  other  topics  as  meat  and  dairy  product
storage.  For serious gardeners.

509.   Bubel, Mike, and Nancy Bubel.  ROOT CELLARING: THE
SIMPLE NO-PROCESSING WAY TO STORE FRUITS AND
VEGETABLES.  Emmaus, PA: Rodale Press, 1979.  297p.
The  proper  storage of fruit  and  vegetables  in
basement  root  cellars,  in  free-standing  root
cellars,  and  other storage areas is  described
in  this title.  Requirements for proper  storage
and  construction methods for  storage  facilities
are  fully  described.  Also  included  are
discussions of which vegetables and which specific
varieties  are better for storage,  how to harvest
and prepare for storage,  and also about 40  pages
of recipes.

## Famous Gardeners on Gardening

(Gardening  literature is enjoyable to read!  The
following  are  writers  on  gardening  which  are
personal  favorites of this compiler.  Of  course
there  are many more,  including some such as  Mr.
Everett  (38),  treated  elsewhere  in  this
bibliography.)

510.   Jekyll, Gertrude.  GERTRUDE JEKYLL ON GARDENING.
Penelope Hobhouse, ed.  Boston: David R. Godine,
1984.  336P.
Gertrude  Jekyll  was  one  of  England's  most
influential  gardeners and garden designers in the
early  twentieth century.  Although she  designed
only a few gardens outside of England,  her  books
on many aspects of gardening were very popular and
influential throughout the gardening world.  Many
of  these  titles  have recently  been  reprinted.
This  title  features selected excerpts  from  her
works  and  follows a  month-by-month  chronology,
taking the reader through a gardening  year.  The
editor  states,  "I  have quoted her  writings  on
plants  and  planting rather than  discussing  her
role  as  a  designer."  It  makes  an  excellent
introduction to Miss Jekyll's garden philosophy.

511.   Sackville-West, Vita.  V. SACKVILLE-WEST'S GARDEN BOOK.
Philippa Nicolson, ed.  New York: Atheneum,

1969.  250p.

Vita Sackville-West's gardening titles are filled with personal observation on many choice and unusual plants. She and her husband, Harold Nicolson, created the famous garden at Sissinghurst in England. This anthology taken from four of her garden books is a good introduction to her garden writings. The arrangment follows a garden throughout the year. Read what she says about sweet woodruff or about a thyme lawn to find why she has been so popular with gardeners. Another aspect of Sackville-West's writings on gardening is found in her beautiful long poem, THE GARDEN.

512.  Gerard, John.  THE HERBAL; OR GENERAL HISTORY OF PLANTS.  New York: Dover Pub., 1975.  1678p.

This famous title was reprinted by Dover and is a reproduction of the 1633 (second) edition. It is written in beautiful Elizabethan prose and Mr. Gerard's observations on plants and gardening still make fascinating reading. In his preface he states, "What greater delight is there than to behold the earth apparelled with plants as with a robe of embroidered works, set with Orient pearls and garnished with great diversitie of rare and costly jewels? But these delights are in the outward senses. The principle delight is in the minde, singularly enriched with the knowledge of these visible things, setting forth to us the invisible wisdome and admirable workmanship of almighty God." Or perhaps this experience shared by many gardeners throughout the ages, "I received two plants that prospered exceeding well; the one whereof I bestowed upon a learned apothecary of Colchester, which continueth to this day bearing both floures and ripe seed. But an ignorant weeder of my garden plucked mine up and cast it away in my absence instead of a weed, by which mischance I am not able to write hereof so absolutely as I determinded."

513.  Beston, Henry.  HERBS AND THE EARTH.  Garden City, NY: Doubleday, 1935.  144p.

The importance of herbs and gardening throughout the ages and to Mr. Beston, one of America's great naturalists, are recorded in this classic title. The author states, "It is only when we are aware of the earth and of the earth as poetry that

we truly live," and again, "A garden is the mirror
of a mind.  It is a place of life, a mystery of
green moving to the pulse of the year, and
pressing on and pausing the whole to its own
inherent rhythms."  A book for gardeners to read,
ponder and cherish.

514.   Jefferson, Thomas.  THOMAS JEFFERSON'S GARDEN BOOK.
Edwin Morris Betts, ed.  Philadephia: American
Philosophical Society, 1944.  704p.
How better to understand the importance of
gardening in early America and specifically to
Thomas Jefferson, than to read this anthology.
Included are Jefferson's writings in his garden
book from 1766 to 1824 and many other writings and
letters pertaining to gardening.  Planting lists
and seeds solicited by Jefferson from Europe are
among the topics included.

515.   White, Katharine S.  ONWARD AND UPWARD IN THE GARDEN.
New York: Farrar, Straus, Giroux, 1979.  361p.
Katherine White's occasional column in THE NEW
YORKER was welcomed by gardeners and also by
connoisseurs of good prose.  She wrote on many
diverse subjects such as gardening catalogs,
garden literature, flower arranging, and much
more.  The fourteen essays reprinted here are not
indexed.

516.   Thomas, Graham Stuart.  THE ART OF PLANTING.  Boston:
David R. Godine, 1984.  323p.
A lifetime experience with plants by Mr. Thomas
has given us this information filled volume that
should be at the gardener's hand whenever he/she
is garden planning.  His early chapters try to
define the history of garden planting in England
along with the use of color, texture, perspective,
and styles of planting.  His second part defines
what the major groupings of plants can do for the
landscape, while the third section defines garden
fragrance, use of water, hedges, etc.  The last
section lists plants for specific purposes such as
large-leaved plants, grey-leaved plants, those
having autumn color and much more.  Here many
detailed lists are used.  Appended is a
chronological yearly list of plants of interest.
For serious gardeners this could be one of their
most consulted gardening titles.

517.   Fox, Helen M.  ADVENTURE IN MY GARDEN.  New York:
Crown Pub., 1965.  167p.

One of America's famous gardeners, this title on
general gardening has been very popular. Again as
in many of these   personal gardening titles,   it
follows the author in her garden season by season.
This title has charm and also good gardening
advice. Her other books on herbs and lilies are
as enjoyable.

518.  McMahon, Bernard. McMAHON'S ANERICAN GARDENER.
      11th ed. New York: Funk & Wagnalls, 1976.
      Reprint of 1857 edition. 637p.
      Mr. McMahon's gardening manual became one of most
      influential garden titles of the early nineteenth
      century. The first edition was published in
      Philadelphia in 1806 and as Elisabeth Woodburn
      states (7), it "set a standard for the full scale
      treatment of horticulture." The eleventh edition
      was the last edition published. Gardeners will be
      amazed at the many varieties of plants that were
      available to that century's gardeners.

519.  Nuese, Josephine. THE COUNTRY GARDEN. New York:
      Scribner, 1970. 256p.
      This title is for many gardeners a favorite
      armchair garden book. It is a great book to
      occasionally pick up to savor her   fine prose.
      Her first sentence gives an indication of the joys
      of this title, "Anyone who thinks that gardening
      begins in the spring and ends in the fall is
      missing the best part of the whole year. For
      gardening begins in January, begins with the
      dream." This title is again arranged month by
      month.

520.  Lloyd, Christopher. THE WELL-TEMPERED GARDEN.
      New York: Dutton, 1970. 485p.
      One of the most popular modern English gardening
      titles is this general gardening manual by
      Christopher Lloyd. Good advice is   given on
      plant selection for many areas of the landscape.
      Although he includes good cultural and design
      advice, his descriptions of the diverse plant
      material available to English gardeners make
      American gardeners enjoy this book. It might be
      frustrating to novice gardeners as many of the
      plants described are unavailable in North America.

521.  Sarton, May. PLANT DREAMING DEEP. New York:
      W.W. Norton, 1968. 189p.
      Admirers of Miss Sarton's journals, poetry and
      novels, as well as gardeners will enjoy this book.

Gardening and plants are prominent in many of her other titles as well.

522. THE GARDENER'S WORLD. Joseph Wood Krutch, ed. New York: Putnam, 1959. 476p.

There are many anthologies of writings on gardening, but Mr. Krutch's compilation is probably the best. Essays on the pleasures of gardening, exploring for plants, and many other subjects are included. Writers include Thoreau, Walpole, Linnaeus, Melville, Darwin, and Virgil.

523. Swain, Roger B. EARTHLY PLEASURES: TALES FROM A BIOLOGIST'S GARDEN. New York: Penguin Books, 1985. 198p.

Entertaining and informational, most gardeners will find much in common with Mr. Swain's observations and experiences. Ranging wider afield than gardening, he looks at his total environment. He writes well.

524. Mitchell, Henry. THE ESSENTIAL EARTHMAN: HENRY MITCHELL ON GARDENING. New York: Farrer Straus Giroux, 1983. 244p.

Garden columnist for THE WASHINGTON POST, Mr. Mitchell is one of the best current garden writers. He has strong opinions (if you disagree with him you might call him opinionated), but he is instructive and entertaining. A constant concern of his in this title is the limited variety of plant material available to American gardeners.

## PERIODICALS

### GENERAL GARDENING PERIODICALS
(Listed in order of importance)

525. HORTICULTURE. Horticulture Associates. 755 Boylston St., Boston, MA 02116. Monthly.

This magazine has improved in content and appearance recently. Articles are focused on the amateur gardener and written by recognized national garden authorities. Subjects include ornamental gardening, vegetable gardening, trees and shrubs, and garden design. Monthly features include a column by Roger Swain (523) a garden question and answer column, a book review section, and a sources lists for the plants discussed. This publication is no longer published by The

Massachusetts Horticultural Society but is now privately published.

526. FLOWER AND GARDEN MAGAZINE. Modern Handicraft, 4251 Pennsylvania Ave. Kansas City, MO 64111. Bimonthly.

A general-interest gardening magazine that has been published for over 25 years. Like HORTICULTURE (525), it is designed for beginning gardeners. Among the features are regional columns for eight different climatic gardening areas of the United States, giving bimonthly gardening advice for specific climatic areas. New developments in gardening are excellently covered.

527. AMERICAN HORTICULTURIST. American Horticultural Society, Mount Vernon, VA 22121. Monthly.

This publication is published in two alternative monthly formats: a glossy magazine with general articles and a newsletter issue covering news of current happenings in gardening. Both are entitled AMERICAN HORTICULTURIST.

528. PLANTS & GARDENS. Brooklyn Botanic Garden, 1000 Washington Ave., Brooklyn, NY 11225. Quarterly.

Topical issues (called handbooks) are published on many different practical aspects of gardening. Each issue contains short articles written by recognized gardening authorities. One issue a year highlights new happenings in American horticulture with reprinted articles from many gardening publications. Back issues are available from the publisher and make economical sources of topical gardening information.

529. GARDEN DESIGN. American Society of Landscape Architects, 1190 East Broadway, Louisville, KY 40204. Quarterly.

A beautifully produced title on landscape design. Gardens included range from large estate gardens to small intimate gardens. Glossy colored photography and carefully written articles make this a quality publication. Detailed book reviews are included on new landscape design titles. This periodical belongs in many library collections.

530. ORGANIC GARDENING. Rodale Press, Emmaus, PA 18049. Monthly.

Articles on organic gardening, country living, and "healthful" food with recipes are featured. Vegetable gardening and growing herbs and fruit are covered in depth.

531. THE AVANT GARDENER. Horticultural Data Processors,
     Box 489, New York, NY 10028. Monthly.
     Published in newsletter format, this publication
     focuses on what's new in gardening. Practical
     suggestions, new plants, books and tools are
     included. This publication focuses on one aspect
     of gardening in many issues. For serious
     gardeners.

532. PACIFIC HORTICULTURE. The Pacific Horticultural
     Foundation, Hall of Flowers, P.O. Box 22609,
     San Franciso, CA 94122. 4 times a year.
     Certainly of interest to all Western gardeners,
     this quality publication is so well written and
     produced it should be of interest to gardeners
     outside of the West. Besides focusing on the
     plants that will grow in California, it contains
     many general articles on famous gardens of the
     world and other articles of historical interest.
     Four California horticultural organizations
     sponsor this publication. One of the best U.S.
     horticultural publications.

533. GARDENS FOR ALL. Gardens for All, 180 Flynn Ave.,
     Burlington, VT 05401. Monthly.
     Vegetable gardening is the focus here. It is
     published in a small newspaper format. A
     practical, how-to-do-it type of publication.

534. THE GARDEN. The Royal Horticultural Society, Vincent
     Square, London SW1P 2PE. Monthly.
     Serious gardeners read this publication of the
     premier horticultural society avidly. Detailed
     gardening articles focus on unusual plant material
     and describe European gardens. Good book reviews
     and evaluations of new cultivars and hybrids of
     many ornamentals, fruits and vegetables are
     included.

535. GARDEN. The Garden Society, Bronx, NY 10458.
     Bimonthly.
     This periodical is co-published for nine
     horticultural organizations (as of 1984)
     throughout the United States and Canada. It
     features nontechnical articles of interest to
     gardeners, amateur botanists, and nature lovers.
     Eight pages of this periodical are printed
     uniquely for each participating institution, while
     the other contents and cover are the same for each
     organization.

536. ARNOLDIA. Arnold Arboretum, The Arborway, Jamaica

Plain, MA. 02130. Quarterly.
Articles on woody plant materials (mostly for the
N.E.) and plant exploration among other topics
will interest gardeners in this quality
publication. It features good photographs and
design.

537.  THE PLANTSMAN. New Perspectives Pub. Ltd., Artists
House, 14-15 Manette St., London W1V 5LB. Quarterly.
Scholarly articles for the serious gardener are
featured in this title sponsored by The Royal
Horticultural Society. Most articles cover
specific genera in depth with careful
descriptions, cultural advice, quality
illustrations and bibliographies. More gardeners
should read this publication on this side of the
Atlantic.

538.  GARDENERS DIGEST. 109 Vanderhoof Ave., Toronto,
Ontario, Canada M4G 2H7. 6 times a year.
A concise general gardening periodical written for
Ontario gardeners. It briefly covers all aspects
of gardening. The articles lack depth. States on
cover: "Canada's only gardening and leisure living
magazine."

539.  CANADIAN GARDEN NEWS. 36 Head St., Dundas, Ontario,
Canada L9H 3H3. 10 times a year.
Described as "a Canadian independent tabloid
newspaper published 10 times a year for the
Canadian amateur gardener" it contains general
interest gardening articles in a tabloid format.
Informally written for the strict amateur.

540.  THE PRAIRIE GARDEN. P.O. Box 517, Winnepeg, Manitoba,
Canada. R3C 2J3. Annual.
"Western Canada's only gardening annual" contains
over 100 pages of interest to gardeners of this
climatic region. Previously titled WINNIPEG
FLOWER GARDEN (1953-54), and THE FLOWER GARDEN
(1955-56).

### PERIODICALS ON SPECIFIC PLANTS
(Divided into outdoor ornamentals, vegetables,
fruit, herbs and indoor plants. The following
plant society publication addresses change
frequently, but these were up-to-date in late
1984. Those interested in other plant societies
and their publications should consult NORTH
AMERICAN HORTICULTURE (1). For those seeking
Canadian publications other than those listed

below should consult: Cole, Trevor, comp.,
CANADIAN SPECIALIST PLANT SOCIETIES.
Publications, Ottawa Research Station,
Agricultural Canada, Central Experimental Farms,
Ottawa, Ontario, Canada K1A OM8.)

## ORNAMENTAL

541. THE CAMELLIA JOURNAL. American Camellia Society,
     Box 1217, Fort Valley, GA 31030. Quarterly.
542. THE CHRYSANTHEMUM. National Chrysanthemum Society,
     % B.L. Markham,2612 Beverly Blvd. S.W., Roanoke,
     VA 24015. Quarterly.
543. THE DAFFODIL JOURNAL. American Daffodil Society.
     Tyner, NC 27980. Quarterly.
544. BULLETIN OF THE AMERICAN DAHLIA SOCIETY. American
     Dahlia Society, % I.B. Owen, 345 Merritt Ave.,
     Bergenfield, NJ 07621. Quarterly.
545. THE DAYLILY JOURNAL. American Hemerocallis Society,
     % J.D. Senior, Route 2, Box 360, DeQueen, AR 71832.
     Quarterly.
 *   FERNS    Cited below as item 567-69.
546. BULLETIN OF THE AMERICAN IRIS SOCIETY. American
     Iris Society, % Mrs. L.D. Stayer, 7414 E. 60th St.
     Tulsa, OK 74145. Quarterly.
547. QUARTERLY BULLETIN OF THE NORTH AMERICAN LILY SOCIETY.
     North American Lily Society, % Mrs. K. Briggs,
     21615 Oxford,Farmington, MI 48024. Quarterly.
548. THE AMERICAN PEONY SOCIETY BULLETIN. American Peony
     Society, % G. Kessenich, 250 Interlachen Rd.,
     Hopkins, MN 55343. Quarterly.
549. PRIMROSES. American Primrose Society, % E. Strickland,
     2722 E. 84th, Tacoma, WA 98445. Quarterly.
550. THE SEED POD. American Hibiscus Society, Drawer 5430,
     Pompano Beach, FL 33064. Quarterly.
551. AMERICAN RHODODENDRON SOCIETY JOURNAL. American
     Rhododendron Society, % F. Egan, 14635 SW Bull Mt.
     Rd., Tigard, OR 97223. Quarterly.
552. BULLETIN OF THE RHODODENDRON SOCIETY OF CANADA. The
     Rhododendron Society of Canada, % Dr. H.G. Hedges,
     4271 Lakeshore Rd., Burlington, Ontario, L7L 1A7.
     2 times a year.
553. BULLETIN OF THE AMERICAN ROCK GARDEN SOCIETY.
     American Rock Garden Society, % N. Singer, SR 66,
     Box 114, Norfolk Rd., Sandisfield, MA 01255. Quarterly
554. THE AMERICAN ROSE MAGAZINE. American Rose Society,
     P.O. Box 30,000, Shreveport, LA 71130. Monthly.

555.  THE CANADIAN ROSE ANNUAL.  The Canadian Rose Society,
      20 Portico Drive, Scarborough, Ontario,
      Canada.  M1G 3R3.  Annual.

                VEGETABLES, FRUIT AND HERBS

*     ORGANIC GARDENING.  Cited above as item 530.
*     GARDENS FOR ALL.  Cited above as item 533.
556.  COMPACT FRUIT TREE.  The International Dwarf Fruit
      Tree Assoc., % R.F. Carlson, 301 Dept. of
      Horticulture, Michigan State U., East Lansing,
      MI 48824.  Bimonthly.
557.  THE NUTSHELL.  Northern Nut Growers Assoc.,
      % S. Chase, 4518 Holston Hills Rd.,
      Knoxville, TN 37914.  Quarterly.
558.  THE HERB GROWER MAGAZINE.  Canaan, CT 06018.
      4 times a year.  Gertrude Foster, editor.
559.  THE HERB QUARTERLY.  Box 275, Newfane, VT 05345.
      Quarterly.

                       INDOOR PLANTS

560.  THE BEGONIAN.  American Begonia Society.  % P. Benell,
      10331 S. Colima Rd, Whittier, CA 90604.  Bimonthly.
561.  INTERNATIONAL BONSAI.  Wm. N. Valavanis,
      412 Pinnacle Rd., Rochester, NY 14623.  Quarterly.
562.  BONSAI BULLETIN.  The Bonsai Society of Greater
      New York, P.O. Box 154, Malverne, NY 11565.
      Quarterly.
563.  BONSAI JOURNAL.  American Bonsai Society, % A. Moyle,
      Keene, NH 03431.  Quarterly.
564.  JOURNAL OF THE BROMELIAD SOCIETY.  The Bromeliad
      Society, P.O. Box 189, La Mirada, CA 90637.
      6 times a year.
565.  CACTUS AND SUCCULENT JOURNAL.  Cactus and Succulent
      Society of America, Box 3010, Santa Barbara,
      CA 93130.  Bimonthly.
*     THE CAMELLIA JOURNAL.  Cited above as item 541.
566.  ELVIN McDONALD'S PLANTER.  Elvin McDonald, 225 E.
      57th St., New York, NY 10022.  24 times a year.
567.  LOS ANGELES INTERNATIONAL FERN SOCIETY JOURNAL.
      Los Angeles International Fern Society,
      % O.J. Myers, 14895 Gardenhill Drive,
      La Mirada, CA 90638.  10 times a year.
568.  FIDDLEHEAD FORUM.  The American Fern Society,

% Dr. L.G. Hickok, Dept. of Botany, U. of Tennessee,
Knoxville, TN 37916. 6 times a year.
569. AMERICAN FERN JOURNAL. The American Fern Society,
% Dr. L.G. Hickok, Dept. of Botany, U. of Tennessee,
Knoxville, TN 37916. Quarterly.
570. GERANIUMS AROUND THE WORLD. International Geranium
Society, % Mrs. B. Tufenkian, 4610 Druid St.,
Los Angeles, CA 90032. Quarterly.
571. GESNERIAD SAINTPAULIA NEWS. Gesneriad Society
International, and Saintpaulia International.
% The Indoor Gardener Pub., 1800-1802 Grand Ave,
P.O. Box 549, Knoxville, TN 37901. Bimonthly.
572. AFRICAN VIOLET MAGAZINE. African Violet Society of
America, Box 1326, Knoxville, TN 37901.
5 times a year.
573. THE GLOXINIAN. American Gloxinia and Gesneriad
Society, % E.M. Todd, P.O. Box 493, Beverly Farms,
MA 01915. 6 times a year.
574. THE INDOOR GARDEN. Indoor Gardening Society of
America, % R.D. Morrison, 5305 S.W. Hamilton St.,
Portland, OR 97221. 6 times a year. (formerly
The Indoor Light Gardening Society of America).
575. AMERICAN ORCHID SOCIETY BULLETIN. American Orchid
Society, 6000 S. Olive Ave., West Palm Beach,
FL 33405. Monthly.
576. THE ORCHID DIGEST. The Orchid Digest Corp.,
% Mrs. N.H. Atkinson, P.O. Box 916, Carmichael,
CA 95608. Bimonthly.
577. THE ORCHID REVIEW. The Orchid Review Ltd.,
% W. Rittershausen, 5 Orchid Ave., Kingsteignton,
Newton Abbot, Devon TQ12 3HG. Monthly.
578. THE CANADIAN ORCHID JOURNAL. The Canadian Orchid
Journal Society, P.O. Box 9472, Station 'B',
St. John's, Newfoundland, Canada A1A 2Y4. Quarterly.


PERIODICALS OF REGIONAL INTEREST
(many of these periodicals have merits outside of
their geographic concerns, but are listed here
because they also contain articles of particular
regional interest)

NORTHEASTERN U.S.

579. THE GREEN SCENE. Pennsylvania Horticultural Society,
325 Walnut St., Philadelphia, PA 19106. Bimonthly.

SOUTHERN SUBTROPICAL

580.  FAIRCHILD TROPICAL GARDEN BULLETIN.  Fairchild Tropical
      Garden, 10901 Old Cutler Rd., Miami, FL 33156.
      Quarterly.

MIDWEST

581.  THE MORTON ARBORETUM QUARTERLY.  Morton Arboretum,
      Lisle, IL 60532. Quarterly.
582.  THE MINNESOTA HORTICULTURIST.  Minnesota Horticultural
      Society, 161 Alderman Hall, 1970 Folwell Ave.,
      St. Paul, MN 55108.  9 times a year.
583.  MISSOURI BOTANICAL GARDEN BULLETIN.  Missouri
      Botanical Garden, 4344 Shaw Blvd., St. Louis,
      MO 63110.  7 times a year.

ROCKY MOUNTAIN STATES

584.  THE GREEN THUMB.  Denver Botanic Gardens, 909 York St.,
      Denver, CO 80206.  Quarterly. (also publish
      a monthly NEWSLETTER).
  *   SUNSET.  Cited below as item 585.

WESTERN U.S.

  *   PACIFIC HORTICULTURE.  Cited above as 532.
585.  SUNSET.  Lane Pub., Menlo Park, CA 94025.  Monthly.
      (has special regional editions).
586.  CALIFORNIA GARDEN.  San Diego Floral Assoc.,
      Casa del Prado, Balboa Park, San Diego, CA 92101.
      Bimonthly.

CANADA

587.  PAPPUS.  Royal Botanical Gardens.  Box 399,
      Hamilton, Ontario, Canada, L8N 3H8.  Quarterly.

      PROFESSIONAL AND PLANT SOCIETIES PUBLICATIONS
        (see addresses under periodical listings)

  *   American Horticultural Society.  NORTH AMERICAN
      HORTICULTURE: A REFERENCE GUIDE.  see (1).
      Council on Botanical and Horticultural Libraries.
        Bibliographies.
          This  professional  library  organization  has
        routinely  published bibliographies of interest to
        gardeners.   More recent titles are listed  below,
        but  there  are many older bibliographies in  this

series that would be of interest.
588. McKiernan, Gerard. DESERT GARDENING. (#1)
589. Schwartz, Diane. VEGETABLE COOKERY. (#2)
590. Schwartz, Diane. EDIBLE WILD PLANTS. (#3)
591. Schofield, Eileen K. BOTANICAL CRAFTS. (#4)
592. Zanoni, Thomas, and Schofield, Eileen K. DYES
     FROM PLANTS. (#5)
593. Miasek, Meryl A., and Long, Charles R.
     ENDANGERED PLANT SPECIES. (#6)
594. Richardson, Mick. HALLUCINOGENIC PLANTS. (#7)


Professional and Plant Society Publications

Royal Horticultural Society.

595. DAFFODILS: A NEW LIST OF DAFFODIL NAMES
     REGISTERED SINCE 1960 WITH COLOUR CODING.
596. DAHLIAS: TENTATIVE CLASSIFICATION LIST AND
     INTERNATIONAL REGISTER OF DAHLIA NAMES 1969.
597. DELPHINIUMS: A TENTATIVE LIST OF DELPHINIUM
     NAMES AND SUPPLEMENT 1970.
598. DIANTHUS: THE FIRST INTERNATIONAL CHECK LIST FOR
     PINKS AND CARNATIONS 1974.
 *   ORCHIDS. Cited above as item 412.
599. THE LILY REGISTER.
600. RHODODENDRONS, CAMELLIAS AND MAGNOLIAS 1980/81.
601. RHODODENDRONS, CAMELLIAS AND MAGNOLIAS 1981/82.
602. THE RHODODENDRON HANDBOOK.
603. RHODODENDRON SPECIES, AN ALPHABETICAL CHECKLIST.
     (also lists many other publications for sale).

American Camellia Society.

604. AMERICAN CAMELLIA YEARBOOK.

National Chrysanthemum Society.

605. BEGINNER'S HANDBOOK.
606. BREEDER'S HANDBOOK.
607. ADVANCED GROWER'S HANDBOOK.
608. SHOW AND JUDGES' HANDBOOK.
609. CHRYSANTHEMUM CLASSIFICATION HANDBOOK.
610. CARE OF STOCK PLANTS-ROOTED CUTTINGS.
611. CHRYSANTHEMUM CULTURE IN THE HOME GARDEN.
612. THE NOVICE EXHIBITOR.

American Daffodil Society.

613. DAFFODILS TO SHOW AND GROW.
614. HANDBOOK FOR GROWING, EXHIBITING, AND JUDGING DAFFODILS.
615. THE DAFFODIL HANDBOOK.
616. THE PRINT-OUT OF DAFFODIL DATA BANK.
617. AMERICAN DAFFODIL SOCIETY APPROVED LIST OF MINIATURES.
618. DAFFODILS IN IRELAND.
       (also have R.H.S. Daffodil yearbooks for sale).

American Hemerocallis Society.

619. BEGINNER'S HANDBOOK.
620. HEMEROCALLIS CHECK LIST (July 1, 1973 to
       December 31, 1983).

American Iris Society.

*   THE WORLD OF IRISES.   Cited above as item 174.
621. BASIC IRIS CULTURE.
622. IRISES FOR EVERYONE.
623. 1959 IRIS CHECKLIST.
624. 1979 IRIS CHECKLIST.
625. REGISTRATIONS AND INTRODUCTIONS. yearly. 1977-.

The North American Liliy Society.

626. YEARBOOK.
627. HYBRID LILY LISTS.
628. LILY DISEASES.
629. LILY DEALERS LIST.
630. GROWING LILIES FROM SEED.
631. SHOW MANUAL.

American Peony Society.

632. PEONIES: A HISTORY OF PEONIES AND THEIR ORIGINATIONS.
       Ed. by Greta M. Kessenich.
633. HANDBOOK OF THE PEONY. 4th ed.
634. THE PEONIES. Edited by J.C. Wister.

American Rock Garden Society.
(offer their own publications and many  more,  see
back cover of their BULLETIN (553).

American Hibiscus Society.

635. WHAT EVERY HIBISCUS GROWER SHOULD KNOW.

American Rhododendron Society.
(offer their own publications and many more, see their JOURNAL (551).

American Rose Society.

636. AMERICAN ROSE ANNUAL.
637. HANDBOOK FOR SELECTING ROSES.

North American Nut Growers Assoc.

 *   NUT TREE CULTURE IN NORTH AMERICA.  Cited above as item
     346.

American Begonia Society.
(offer their own publications and many  more,  see
THE BEGONIAN (560).

International Bonsai Arboretum.
(offers many imported Japanese titles).

Bromeliad Society.

638. BROMELIADS: A CULTURAL HANDBOOK.
639. A GLOSSARY FOR BROMELIAD GROWERS.
640. CHECKLIST OF BROMELIAD HYBRIDS.
641. HANDBOOK FOR JUDGES AND EXHIBITORS.
            (also offers works published elsewhere).

American Gloxinia and Gesneriad Soceity.

642. FLOWER SHOW MANUAL.
643. CULTURE LEAFLETS.
644. LEARN HOW TO PROPAGATE FAVORITE GESNERIADS.

African Violet Society of America.

645. HANDBOOK FOR JUDGES AND EXHIBITORS.
646. MINIATURES & SEMIMINIATURE VARIETY LIST.

Indoor Garden Society.

647. Morrison, Pat.  LEARN TO GROW UNDER FLUORSCENT LIGHTS.
648. Banucci, Phyllis.  LIGHT GARDEN CONSTRUCTION GUIDE.
649. Finkbeiner, Fran.  FERNS UNDER FLUORESCENTS.
650. Ritzau, Fred.  SEED PROPAGATION UNDER LIGHTS.
651. Kartuz, Michael, and Evelyn Cronin.  FLOWERING
        PLANTS FOR LIGHT GARDENS.

652.  Golding, Jack;  Edward Thompson; and Mildred Thompson.
      BEGONIAS FOR LIGHT GARDENS.
653.  Peterson,  Richard.   ORCHID  CULTURE  UNDER  LIGHTS.

American Orchid Society.

654.  Seibels, Grenville, II.  HANDBOOK ON ORCHID PHOTOGRAPHY.
655.  HANDBOOK ON JUDGING AND EXHIBITING.
656.  HANDBOOK ON ORCHID CULTURE.
      (numerous other publications).


PROFESSIONAL  ORGANIZATIONS  AND NATIONALLY  BASED  GARDEN
CLUB ORGANIZATIONS THAT ARE OF INTEREST TO GARDENERS

657.  AMERICAN ASSOCIATION OF BOTANICAL GARDENS AND
      ARBORETA, P.O. Box 206, Swarthmore, PA 19081.
658.  AMERICAN ASSOCIATION OF NURSERYMEN, 230 Southern Bldg.,
      Washington, DC 20005.
659.  AMERICAN SOCIETY FOR HORTICULTURAL SCIENCE,
      701 North Saint Asaph Street, Alexandria, VA 22314.
660.  THE AMERICAN SOCIETY OF LANDSCAPE ARCHITECTS,
      1733 Connecticut Ave. N.W., Washington, DC 20009.
661.  THE COUNCIL ON BOTANICAL AND HORTICULTURAL LIBRARIES,
      % New York Botanical Garden, Bronx, NY 10458.
662.  GARDEN WRITERS ASSOC. OF AMERICA, Box 10221,
      Fort Wayne, IN 46851.
663.  INTERNATIONAL SOCIETY OF ARBORICULTURE, Box 71,
      Urbana, IL 61801.
664.  NATIONAL COUNCIL FOR THERAPY AND REHABILITATION THROUGH
      HORTICULTURE, 9041 Comprint, Suite #103, Gaithersburg,
      MD 20877.
665.  NATIONAL COUNCIL OF STATE GARDEN CLUBS, 4401
      Magnolia Ave., St. Louis, MO 63110.
666.  THE GARDEN CLUB OF AMERICA, 598 Madison Ave.,
      New York, NY 10022.
667.  MEN'S GARDEN CLUBS OF AMERICA, INC., 5560 Merle Hay Rd.,
      Des Moines, IA 50323.


SEED AND NURSERY CATALOGS
(This  is a selected  listing.  For more  catalogs
consult the following references to seed catalogs.
Also, many advertise in plant society publications
and   are  often  listed  in  appendixes  of  many
gardening books.  The catalogs included here  are
listed  in order of the breakdown of plant material
in this bibliography. Starred items indicate there

is a charge for the catalog.)

REFERENCES TO CATALOGS

668. "Nursery Source Guide." PLANTS & GARDENS. Brooklyn:
     Brooklyn Botanic Garden, 1977. vol 33, No. 2.
       A  selected  guide  to  1200  trees  and  shrubs.
     Sources for species and cultivars are given  along
     with  brief  descriptions  of  the  plants.   Both
     retail  and  wholesale sources  are  listed.   The
     listing  is  classified by broad type of  tree  or
     shrub.

669. "Sources of Shade Trees in the United States-1983."
     Wooster, OH: Ohio State U./Ohio Agr. Research &
     Development Center, 1983. Special Circular 105
     (revised).
       Trees  are  listed  alphabetically by  genus  with
     common names cross referenced to scientific  names
     in this source list.   The many sources are listed
     by  state  and  the firm's name.   Appended  is  a
     listing  of names and addresses  of  participating
     nurseries arranged by state.

670. NURSERY SOURCES FOR NATIVE PLANTS AND WILDFLOWERS.
     Framington, MA: New England Wild Flower Society,
     1981.
       A  listing  of 204 nurseries in the United  States
     and Canada which offer native plant material.   The
     listing  is  divided  into  nurseries  selling
     perennial native plants,  woody plants,  seeds, and
     a miscellaneous grouping.   Indications of whether
     material  is propagated or collected  and  whether
     the nursery ships is included.   It is not a guide
     to  sources  of  specific  wildflowers  or  native
     plants.

671. COMBINED ROSE LIST 1985.  Compiled and available
     from: Beverly R. Dobson, 215 Harriman Rd.,
     Irvington, NY 10533.
       After  a  listing  of names and addresses  of  the
     source  nurseries,   this  gives  sources  of
     alphabetically arranged rose hybrids and species.

672. THE GARDEN SEED INVENTORY.  [Available from Seed
     Savers Exchange, 203 Rural Ave., Decorah, IA 52101.]
     Described as listing sources for nearly 6,000 non-
     hybrid varieties of vegetable seeds.

673. Spatzek, Jim.  ORCHID SPECIES SOURCE BOOK II.
     [Available from Twin Oak Books.  See listing of
     book dealers].

Over 100 suppliers of orchid species are included
in this guide to orchid species. It is arranged
alphabetically by genus. It states it contains
over 4,400 species from over 400 genera.

## WATER GARDEN PLANTS

674. Lilyponds Water Gardens. 6800 Lilypons Rd.,
     P.O. Box 10, Lilypons, MD 21717-0010.
675. William Tricker. 74 Allendale Ave., P.O. Box 398,
     Saddle River, NJ 07458.

## WILDFLOWERS & FERNS

676. Putney Nursery. Putney, VT 05346. Wildflowers, ferns,
     and few perennials.
677. *Siskiyou Rare Plant Nursery. 2835 Cummings Rd.,
     Medford, OR 97501. Wildflowers, alpines,
     rock gardening plants.
678. Gardens of the Blue Ridge. P.O. Box 10, Pineola,
     NC 28662. Wildflowers, native trees, shrubs,
     bulbs, ferns.
679. Illini Gardens. P.O. Box 125, Oakford, IL 62673.
     Wildflowers, ferns, perennials.
680. Clyde Robin Seed Co. P.O. Box 2855, Castro Valley,
     CA 94546. Wildflower seeds.

## ROCK GARDEN PLANTS

 *   *Siskiyou Rare Plant Nursery. Cited above as item 677.
681. Stonecrop Nurseries. Rt 301, Cold Spring, NY 10516.
     Alpines, rock garden plants, perennials.
682. Rakestraw's Perennial Gardens & Nursery. G-3094 S.
     Term St., Burton, MI 48529. Hardier rock garden
     plants, conifers.
683. *Carroll Gardens. Box 310, 444 East Main St.,
     Westminster, MD 21157. Perennials, rock garden
     plants, herb plants, etc.

## GENERAL NURSERY CATALOGS

684. *Wayside Gardens. Hodges, SC 29695. Spring & Fall
     catalogs. Beautiful color photographs. Especially
     valuable for perennials.
685. *White Flower Farm. Litchfield, CT 06759-0050.
     Spring & Fall catalogs. Good for choice perennials.
686. Gossler Farms Nursery. 1200 Weaver Rd., Springfield,

OR 97478-9663. Unusual woody ornamentals,
especially Magnolia.
687. Girard Nurseries. P.O. Box 428, Geneva, OH 44041.
Woody ornamentals. Rhododendrons.
688. *Monrovia Nursery Co. P.O. Box Q, 18331 East Foothill
Blvd., Azusa, CA 91702. Woody ornamentals.
California plants. Wholesale only.
689. *Weston Nurseries. Hopkinton, MA 01748. Unusual
woody ornamentals, fruits, nuts, perennials, roses.
690. *Princeton Nurseries. P.O. Box 191, Princeton, NJ
08540. Woody ornamentals. Wholesale.
691. Lake County Nursery Exchange. Route 84, Box 122,
Perry, OH 44081. Woody ornamentals. Wholesale.
692. Miller Nurseries. Canandaigua, NY 14424. Fruit,
nuts, a few trees and shrubs.
693. Kelley Bros. Nurseries. Dansville, NY 14437. Fruit,
nuts, trees, shrubs, a few perennials.
694. Farmer Seed and Nursery. Faribault, MN 55021.
Vegetable seeds, hardier varieties of fruit, trees,
shrubs, roses, perennials.
695. Henry Field Seed & Nursery. Shenandoah, IA 51602.
Vegetable seeds, fruit, nuts, trees, shrubs,
perennial, etc.
696. Musser Forests. Box 340M, Indiana, PA 15701-0340.
Seedling and small transplants of trees and shrubs.
697. Dilatush Nursery. 780 Route 130, Robbinsville, NJ
08691. Unusual woody plants, Japanese maples,
ornamental grasses.
698. Dauber's Nurseries. P.O. Box 1746, York, PA 17405.
Unusual woody plants.
699. Upper Bank Nurseries. P.O. Box 486, Media, PA 19063.
Woody plants, bamboo.
700. Heard Gardens. 5355 Merle Hay Rd., Des Moines, IA
50323. Lilacs.
701. Heaths and Heathers. P.O. Box 850, Elma, WA 98541.
100 varieties.
702. The Bovees Nursery. 1737 S.W. Coronado St.,
Portland, OR 97219. Rhododendron. Other woody
ornamentals, rock garden plants.
703. *Baldsiefen Nursery. Box 88, Bellvale, NY 10912.
Rhododendron.
704. Van Veen Nursery. 4201 S.E. Franklin St., Box 06444,
Portland, OR 9706. Rhododendron.

## CLEMATIS

705. *Blackthorne Gardens. 48 Quincy St., Holbrook,

MA 02343–1898.

## PERENNIALS

*   Wayside Gardens. Cited above as item 684.
*   White Flower Farm. Cited above as item 685.
706.   Holbrook Farm & Nursery. Route 2, Box 223B, Fletcher, NC 28732. Perennials, dwarf woody plants, wildflowers, ferns.
707.   Garden Place. 6776 Heisley Rd, Box 388, Mentor, OH 44061–0388. Perennials.
*   Carroll Gardens. Cited above as item 683.
708.   Bluestone Perennials. 7211 Middle Ridge Rd., Madison, OH 44057. Perennials.
709.   Huff's Gardens. P.O. Box 187, Burlington, KS 66839. Chrysanthemum.
710.   Blue Dahlia Gardens. San Jose, IL 6282. Dahlias.
711.   Swan Island Dahlias. Box 800, Canby, OR 97013. Dahlias.
712.   *Gilbert H. Wild. Sarcoxie, MO 64862. Daylilies, iris, peonies.
713.   *Borbeleta Gardens. 10078 154th Ave., Elk River, MN 55330–6223. Daylilies, lilies.
714.   *Cooley's Gardens. Box 126, Silverton, OR 97381. Iris.
715.   Brand Peony Farm. Box 842, St. Cloud, MN 56302. Peonies, iris, daylilies.
716.   Louis Smirnow. P.O. Box 251, Glen Head, Long Island, NY 11545. Tree peonies.
717.   Far North Gardens. 16785 Harrison, Livonia, MI 48154. Primrose seed, much more.
718.   Jackson & Perkins. Medford, OR 97501. Roses, fruit, trees, etc.
719.   Nor'East Miniature Roses. 58 Hammond St., Rowley, MA 01969. Miniature roses.
720.   Roses of Yesterday and Today. 802 Brown's Valley Rd., Wastsonville, CA 95076–0398. Historic roses.
721.   Armstrong Nurseries. P.O. Box 4060, Ontario, CA 91761. Roses, fruit.

## BULBS

722.   John Scheepers, Inc. 63 Wall St. New York, NY 10005.
723.   P. de Jager & Sons. P.O. Box 100, Brewster, NY 10509.
724.   Howard B. French. Rt 100, Pittsfield, VT 05762–0565.
*   White Flower Farm. Cited above as item 685.

725. Noweta Gardens.  St. Charles, MN 55972.  Gladiolus.
726. *Rex Bulb Farms.  P.O. Box 774 Port Townsend,
     WA 98368. Lilies.
  *  Blackthorne Gardens.  Cited above as item  705.
     Lilies, misc. bulbs.
  *  Borbeleta Gardens.  Cited above as item 713.  Lilies,
     narcissus, iris.
727. Grant E. Mitsch Novelty Daffodils.  Mr. & Mrs. R.D.
     Havens, P.O. Box 218, Hubbard, OR 97032. Narcissus.
728. Daffodil Mart.  Rt 3, Box 794, Gloucester, VA 23061.

## ORNAMENTAL GRASSES & BAMBOO

729. Kurt Bluemel, 2543 Hess Rd., Fallston, MD 21047.
     Ornamental grass.
  *  Dilatush Nursery.  Cited above as  item  697.
     Ornamental grass.
730. American Bamboo Company.  345 W. Second St., Dayton,
     OH 45402. 2 hardier outdoor varieties of bamboo.
  *  Upper Bank Nurseries.  Cited above as item 699.
     Bamboo.

## FRUIT

  *  J.E. Miller Nurseries.  Cited above as item 692.
     Fruit, nuts.
  *  Kelly Bros. Nurseries.  Cited above as item 693.
     Fruit, nuts.
731. Southmeadow Fruit Gardens.  2363 Tilbury Place,
     Birmingham, MI 48009. Large selection of fruit
     varieties, some rare varieties.
732. Emlong Nurseries.  Stevensville, MI 49127.
     Hardier fruit, nuts.
733. Stark Bro's Nurseries & Orchards.  Louisiana, MO
     63353-0010. Fruit, nuts.
  *  Henry Field's.  Cited above as item 695.  Fruit, nuts.
  *  Farmer Seed & Nursery.  Cited above as item 694.
     Fruit, nuts.
  *  Armstrong.  Cited above as item 721.  Fruit, nuts.
  *  Jackson & Perkins.  Cited above as item 718.  Fruit.
734. Buntings' Nurseries.  Selbyville, DE 19975.
     Strawberries, other fruit, nuts.
735. The Conner Company.  105 North Second St.,
     P.O. Box 534, Augusta, AR 72006.  Strawberries.

SEEDS
(vegetable, flower, herb, houseplant, etc.)

736.  Park Seed Co.  Hwy. 254 N., Greenwood, SC 29647.
      Flower, vegetable, houseplant, herb seeds;
      houseplants, bulbs, etc.
737.  W. Atlee Burpee.  Warminster, PA 18974.  Vegetable,
      flower, herb seeds, fruits, nuts, misc.
738.  Joseph Harris Co.  Moreton Farm, 3670 Buffalo Rd.,
      Rochester, NY 14624.  Vegetable, flower.
739.  Stokes Seeds.  Box 548, Buffalo, NY 14240.
      Vegetable, flower.
740.  Thompson & Morgan.  P.O Box 100, Farmingdale,
      NJ 07727.  North America outlet of English firm
      specializing in European flower and vegetable
      seeds.
  *   Farmer Seed & Nursery.  Cited above as item 694.
      Hardier vegetables, seed potato eyes.
  *   Henry Field.  Cited above as item 695.  Vegetable,
      few flower.
741.  Nichol's Garden Nursery.  1190 North Pacific Highway,
      Albany, OR 97321.  Herb, unusual vegetable,
      herb plants, etc.
  *   Clyde Robin Seed Co.  Cited above as item 680.
      Wildflower seeds.
742.  *A World Seed Service.  J.L. Hudson.  Box 1058,
      Redwood City, CA 94064.  Inclusive ornamental plant
      seed list, unusual vegetable seeds.
743.  *John Brudy Exotics.  Rt 1, Box 190, Dover, FL 33527.
      Tropical, subtropical, houseplant seeds.
744.  *The Fragrant Path.  P.O. Box 328, Fort Calhoun,
      NE 68023.  Seeds of fragrant, unusual,
      old-fashioned ornamentals, vines.
745.  *The Urban Farmer.  P.O. Box 444, Convent Station,
      NJ 07961.  Unusual vegetables.
746.  Epicure Seeds.  P.O. Box 450, Brewster, NY 10509.
      Unusual vegetables.
747.  Japonica Seeds.  P.O. Box 919, Jackson Heights,
      New York, NY 11372.  Japanese vegetable seeds,
      bonsai seeds.


HERBS

748.  Well Sweep Herb Farm.  317 Mt. Bethel Rd.,
      Port Murray, NJ 07865.  Herb plants & seeds,
      scented geraniums, etc.
  *   Nichol's Garden Nursery.  Cited above as item 741.
      Herb seeds, a few herb plants.
749.  *Sunnybrook Farms Nursery.  9448 Mayfield Rd.,
      P.O. Box 6, Chesterland, OH 44026.  Herb plants,

herb seeds, hostas, scented geraniums, houseplants.
750. Capriland's Herb Farm. Silver St., Coventry, CT 06238.
     Herb seeds & plants, misc.

## HOUSEPLANTS

751. *Logee's Greenhouses. 55 North St., Danielson, CT 06239.
     Houseplants, begonias, geraniums, gesneriads, ferns.
752. Glasshouse Works. 10 Church St., Box 97, Stewart,
     OH 45778-0097. Huge selection of houseplants.
753. *Kartuz Greenhouses. 1408 Sunset Drive, Vista, CA 92083.
     Gesneriads, begonias.
754. The Plant Shop's Botanical Gardens. 18007 Topham St.,
     Reseda, CA 91335. Houseplants, cacti & succulents,
     begonias.
755. The Banana Tree. 715 Northampton St., Easton, PA 18042.
     Rare houseplant seeds, banana plants, misc.
  *  Sunnybrook Farms Nursery. Cited above as item 749.
     Houseplants, begonias, geraniums.
756. Tinari Greenhouses. 2325 Valley Rd., Huntingdon Valley,
     PA 19006. African violets.
757. *Annalee Violetry. 29-50 214th Place, Bayside,
     NY 11360. African violets.
758. *Fischer/McKee's. P.O. Box 96, Northfield, NJ 08225.
     African violets, indoor gardening supplies.
759. The Thompsons. P.O. Drawer PP, Southampton, NY 11968.
     Begonias.
760. Marz Bromeliads. 10782 Citrus Dr., Moorpark, CA 93021.
     Bromeliads, misc. houseplants.
761. Shady Hill Gardens. 821 Walnut St., Batavia,
     IL 60510-2999. Geraniums.
762. Cook's Geranium Nursery. 712 North Grand, Lyons,
     KS 67554. Geraniums.
763. *Abbey Garden Cacti and Succulents. 4620 Carpinteria
     Ave., Carpinteria, CA 93013. Cacti and succulents.
764. *California Epi Center. P.O. Box 1431, Vista, CA 92083.
     Orchid cacti, misc. cacti and succulents.
765. *Singers' Growing Things. 17806 Plummer St.,
     Northridge, CA 91325. Cacti and succulents.
766. Peter Pauls Nurseries. Canandaigua, NY 14424.
     Carnivorous, terrarium plants and supplies.
767. *Black Copper Kits, 266 Kipp St., Hackensack, NJ 07601.
     Carnivorous, terrarium plants and supplies.
768. *Orchids by Hausermann. 2N 134 Addison Rd., Villa Park,
     IL 60181. Orchids.
769. *Penn Valley Orchids. 239 Old Gulph Rd., Wynnewood, PA
     19096. Paphiopedilum, other orchids.

770. *Jones & Scully. 2200 N.W. 33rd Ave., Miami, FL 33142.
     Orchids.
771. Ann Mann's Orchids. Rt 3, Box 202, Orlando,
     FL 32811-9709. Orchids, begonias, bromeliads, many
     misc. houseplants.

## BONSAI SUPPLIES

772. *Western Arboretum's. P.O. Box 2827, Pasadenia,
     CA 91105. Plants, pots, tools.
773. Spring Hollow. 10109 Deal Rd., Williamsburg, MI
     49690. Pots.

## GREENHOUSES

774. Lord & Burnham. P.O. Box 4050, Dept. 10,
     Hicksville, NY 11802.
775. Aluminum Greenhouses. 14605 Lorain Ave.,
     Cleveland, OH 44111.

## GARDENING SUPPLY CATALOGS

776. Kenneth Lynch & Sons. Inc. Wilton, CT 06897.
     Garden accessories and art.
777. A.M. Leonard. 6665 Spiker Rd., Piqua, OH 45356.
778. Smith & Hawken. 25 Corte Madera, Mill Valley,
     CA 94941.
779. *Walter F. Nicke. Box 467G, Hudson, NY 12534.
780. *Charley's Greenhouse Supplies. 12815 N.E. 124th St.
     Kirkland, WA 98033. Greenhouse supplies.
781. *The Necessary Trading Company. Main St., Box 305,
     New Castle, VA 24127. Of interest to organic
     gardeners.
  *  Fischer/McKee's. Cited above as item 758.
782. *Hal Visters Hydroponics. 2640 Harbor Blvd.,
     Costa Mesa, CA 92626. Hydroponics.
783. Indoor Gardening Supplies. P.O. Box 40567,
     Detroit, MI 48240. Indoor light gardening supplies.
784. Tube Craft. 8000 Baker Ave., Cleveland, OH 44102.
     Indoor light gardening units.

       LIBRARIES WITH MAJOR STRENGTHS IN GARDENING
       (College/university libraries are excluded.   See
       the CBHL Directory (3) for other libraries.)

Chicago Botanic Garden Library. P.O. Box 400, Glencoe,
     IL 60022. (312)835-5440 ext 27.

Virginia Henrichs, Librarian.
Civic Garden Center Library. 777 Lawrence Ave. East,
    Don Mills, Ontario, Canada, M3C IP2. (416)445-1552.
    Pamela MacKenzie, Librarian.
Denver Botanic Gardens. Helen Fowler Library. 909 York St.,
    Denver, CO 80206. (303)575-2548. Solange G.
    Gignac, Librarian.
Dumbarton Oaks Garden Library. 1703 32nd St. N.W.,
    Washington, DC 20007. (202)342-3280. Laura Byers,
    Librarian. (Strengths in history of garden design).
Garden Center of Greater Cleveland. Eleanor Squire Library.
    11030 East Blvd., Cleveland, OH 44106. (216)721-1600.
    Richard T Isaacson, Librarian.
Harvard University. Arnold Arboretum and Gray Herbarium
    Libraries. 22 Divinity Ave., Cambridge, MA 02138.
    (617)495-2366. Barbara A. Callahan, Librarian.
Harvard University. Farlow Reference Library.
    20 Divinity Ave., Cambridge, MA 0138.
    (617)495-2369. Geraldine C. Kaye, Librarian.
    (Cryptogamic Botany).
Horticultural Society of New York Library. 128 West
    57th St., New York, NY 10019. (212)757-0915.
    Heidi Friedman, Librarian.
Hunt Institue for Botanical Documentation. Hunt
    Botanical Library. Carnegie-Mellon U., Pittsburgh,
    PA 15213. (412)578-2434. Bernadette G. Callery,
    Librarian. (Major strengths in botanical
    illustration, botanical history).
Kingwood Center Library. 900 Park Ave. West, Mansfield,
    OH 44906. (419)522-0211. Timothy J. Gardner,
    Librarian.
Longwood Gardens, Inc. Library. Kennet Square, PA 19348.
    (215)388-6761 ext. 510. Enola Jane Teeter,
    Librarian.
Los Angeles State and County Arboretum. Plant Science
    Library. 301 N. Baldwin Ave., Arcadia, CA 91006.
    (213)446-8251 ext. 32. Joan DeFato, Librarian.
Massachusetts Horticultural Society. 300 Massachusetts
    Ave., Boston, MA 02115. (617)536-9280.
Minnesota Landscape Arboretum, University.
    Andersen Horticultural Library. 3675 Arboretum Dr.,
    Box 39, Chahassen, MN 55317.(612)443-22460, ext 27.
    June Rogier, Librarian.
Missouri Botanical Garden Library. P.O. Box 299, St. Louis,
    MO 63166. (314)772-7600. Connie Wolf, Librarian.
Morton Arboretum. Sterling Morton Library. Lisle, IL 60532.
    (312)968-0074. Ian MacPhail, Librarian.

New York Botanical Garden Library. Bronx, NY 10458.
    (212)220-8753. Bob Long, Director.
    (Largest N.A. botanical library).
Pennsylvania Horticultural Society Library. 325 Walnut St.,
    Philadelphia, PA 19106. (215)625-8268. Mary Lou
    Wolfe, Librarian.
Royal Botanical Gardens, Hamilton. Library. Box 399,
    Hamilton, Ontario, Canada L8N 3H8. (416)527-1158.
    Ina Vrugtman, Librarian. (Major strengths in Canadian
    garden history).
Smithsonian Institution Libraries. Botany Library.
    10th and Constitutin, Washington, DC 20560.
    (202)357-2715. Ruth F. Schallert, Librarian.
Strybing Arboretum Society. Helen Crocker Russell Library.
    9th Ave. at Lincoln Way, San Francisco, CA 94122.
    (415)661-1316. Jane Gates, Librarian.

GARDENING AND BOTANICAL BOOK DEALERS
    (The following book dealers have been found to be
    knowledgeable    and    to    specialize    in
    gardening/botanical titles.  Many plant societies
    also  offer books of interest to  their  members.
    Also  one  of  the benefits of  belonging  to  The
    Council  on Botanical and Horticultural  Libraries
    (CBHL)  is  to receive duplicate book  lists  from
    member libraries.)

Elisabeth Woodburn. Booknoll Farm, Hopewell, NJ 08525.
Beth L. Bibby - Books. 1225 Sardine Creek Rd., Gold Hill,
    OR 97525.
Pomona Book Exchange. Highway 52, Rockton, Ontario,
    Canada LOR1XO.
Florilegium. Oriel Eaton Kriz. Snedens Landing, Box 157,
    Palisades, NY 10964. A few books, but mainly
    quality botanical prints.
Gary Wayner. Rt 3, Box 18, Fort Payne, AL 35967.
Ian Jackson. P.O. Box 9075, Berkeley, CA 94709.
Hortulus. 101 Scollard St., Toronto, Ontario, Canada M5R 1G4.
Warren F. Broderick - Books. 695 4th Ave., P.O. Box 124,
    Lansingburgh, NY 12182.
Capability's Books. P.O. Box 114, Highway 46, Deer Park,
    WI 54007. New gardening titles.
Timothy Mawson Books. New Preston, CT 06777
John Johnson. Rt 2, North Bennington, VT 05257.
The American Botanist. P.O. Box 143, Brookfield, IL 60513.
Jane Sutley Horticultural Books. 1105 W. Cherry St.,
    Centralia,WA 98531.

Hurley Books.  Westmoreland, NH 03467.
Twin Oaks Books.  4343 Causeway Dr., Lowell, MI 49331.
    Orchid books.
McQuerry Orchid Books.  5700 W. Salerno Rd., Jacksonville,
    FL 32244. Orchid books.

# NAME INDEX

# TITLE INDEX

CLEVELAND BOTANICAL GARDEN

3 4410 00017639 7